Fighter's Fact Book

*Over 400 Concepts, Principles and Drills
to Make You a Better Fighter*

Fighter's Fact Book

*Over 400 Concepts, Principles and Drills
to Make You a Better Fighter*

by
Loren W. Christensen

 Turtle Press   Santa Fe

To contact the author or to order additional copies of this book:
  Turtle Press
  PO Box 34010
  Santa Fe NM 87594-4010
  800-778-8785
  www.turtlepress.com

ISBN 1-880336-37-5
LCCN 00-027249
Printed in the United States of America

19 18 17 16 15 14 13 12 11 10

Library of Congress Cataloguing in Publication Data
Christensen, Loren W.
    Fighter's fact book : over 400 concepts, principles and drills to make you a better fighter / by Loren W. Christensen
        p. cm.
    Includes index.
    ISBN 1-880336-37-5
        1. Martial arts--Training. I. Title.

    GV1102.7.T7 C42 2000
    769.8--dc21   00-027249

Contents

ACKNOWLEDGMENTS

Much love to my wife, Donna, and my children, Carrie, Dan, Amy and Kelly, for their support during my writing projects. I know I'm always hard to live with during those last two drafts.

Thanks to my daughter Amy and Laura Whited for their fine job behind the camera and to all the models who braved the weather and the pain of holding poses.

Donna Christensen
Amy Christensen (1st-degree black belt)
Dan Christensen
Tim Delgman (8th- degree black belt jujitsu)
Gary Sussman (3rd- degree black belt)
Mark Whited (1st- degree black belt)
Jimmy Clark
Daniel Alix (4th- degree black belt)

A special thanks to the following instructors who contributed training tips. Your experience, knowledge and generosity were invaluable in this project.

Instructor Michael Holmes has practiced martial arts for over 15 years. He holds black belts in Nisei Karate-do, Wushu Sansho and Wado-Kai karate. He lives and practices Nisei karate in Vancouver, Canada.

Before settling down to a writing and teaching career, Instructor Marc "Animal" MacYoung worked as a bodyguard, bouncer, event security provider and a director of a correctional institute. As he says, "I'm a man, who despite the best efforts of his enemies, is still breathing." He has taken that experience and has written several books and made numerous videos on the fighting arts.

Instructor Dan Alix, currently a captain in the United States Army, has been training and teaching Tang Soo Do for 20 years. He has also studied karate, taekwondo and hapkido and slants his teaching toward street defense. He is currently stationed on the east coast.

Instructor Bob Orlando has studied aikido, iaido, arnis, and eskrima. However, what has impacted the most is the years he has studied Chinese kuntao and Indonesian pentjak silat under Dutch-Indonesian master William de Thouars.

He still studies with the master today and resides in Colorado.

Instructor Frank Garza has been studying American kenpo karate for many years and is a third-degree black belt under Sifu Rick Fowler. He has also studied, judo, Muay thai, silat, kali and jujitsu. He resides in Texas.

Introduction

In 1965, most of the people in my circle of acquaintances had not heard of karate. "Kar-a- what?" a couple of them asked when I told them I had started taking lessons. "Is that Chinese food or something?" And they weren't trying to be funny. People were somewhat familiar with judo back then, since it had been portrayed in several old World War II movies. But except for a few cities around the country where returning servicemen form Okinawa and Korea had established schools, karate was mostly unheard of.

I remember my first day walking into the Oregon Karate Association and seeing those pajama-clad guys kicking and thrashing all over the training floor. Man, these guys could beat up anybody, I remember thinking in awe.

Although I was a pretty big 19-year-old as a result of lifting weights since I was 13, I had never been good at sports, probably because I wasn't terribly interested in playing them. But something swept over me that first day as I sat along the wall with my mouth hanging open, watching those warriors moving about in their deadly dance. I knew, just as clearly as I knew my name, that karate would be my life. I joined on the spot (monthly dues were only $7 then) and the fighting arts have been part of my life ever since.

That was 1965, and I'm still training in spite of the fact this part of my body really hurts and this other part here doesn't even bend anymore. I'm sure I don't have to tell you that the martial arts can be a little taxing on the ol' bod', especially when you do it decade after decade as I have. But bad shoulder, trick knee, trashed elbow, busted fingers and all my other maladies aside, I wouldn't change a thing that has happened to me during my long martial arts career. They have been wonderful years in which I have met some incredible people (and not just a few weird ones), traveled, taught, and enjoyed a way of life like no other. The fighting arts have kept me in good condition, physically and mentally, and they saved my precious hide many times in the war-torn streets of Saigon during the Vietnam war and in the mean streets of Portland, Oregon where I served 25 years as city police officer.

It's a profound understatement to say that karate has changed since I began. What I teach today and how I teach it is so remote from how and what I learned many moons ago, that it's barely recognizable as being the same. Of course, there are martial arts schools stuck in the ancient past, but most have recognized the need to evolve with the times.

While change isn't always a good thing, there is much that has changed for the good from when I began, for that matter, even in the last five years. New techniques have come along as well as new and better ways to execute basic movements. There have also been new discoveries in ways to train, both physically and mentally. For example, as a white belt, I can remember many classes where we squatted in a deep horse stance and threw hundreds of punches. Did we get good at this? Sure, I developed a tremendous reverse punch. It would be hard not to get proficient at something you do over and over again. But considering the volume of hours that we spent on this ancient exercise, its value as a practical technique is virtually nil. I never once used the horse stance when I sparred in class or in competition, and I definitely never used it in the dozens of street battles I had as a cop. While I did get strong from the exercise, I know now that there are many other ways to develop punching power that are far more interesting, practical and result producing.

Some of the old ways of training were hazardous to one's health, joints, tendons, muscles and ligaments. Today, there are better and safer paths to proficiency, because modern sports medicine and nutrition have invaded the ancient fighting arts and brought sense and science to the way we develop the mind and body.

I'm a strong advocate of using the mind to push beyond what we think is our limit. There are lots of instructors who talk about incorporating the mind in training, competition and self-defense, but they speak of it in mystical terms that leave their students wondering what the heck they are talking about. Many times students don't understand because the instructor doesn't understand either. All too often, he is trying to sound like a white-bearded sage sitting in the lotus position on the peak of Japan's Mt. Fuji. This is unfortunate because there is no need for confusion and mysticism in this area of training. Learning to incorporate the mind in karate training should be no more complex than throwing a reverse punch.

It's good when students are loyal to an instructor and to a fighting style, but it's not good when they blindly follow whatever the instructor tells them. I did that and wasted my first three years of training. But I didn't have much to compare it to then because information on the fighting arts was sparse. Today's students, however, live in the information age. There is no reason to lack knowledge of techniques and training ideas when there is such a plethora of educational material available everywhere you look. There are now thousands of schools in the United States, making this country a melting pot of martial arts instruction. Additionally, there are many excellent books (ahem . . . like this one), instructional videos, magazines, CD roms, and Jackie Chan movies (just kidding about Jackie Chan). Getting these instructional aids will educate you and open your eyes to the truth. The more enlightened you are, the more easily you will see what is valid and the more intelligent will be the questions you ask in your search for even more knowledge.

It's my hope that you find this book to be an encyclopedia of training and fighting ideas no matter what karate discipline you follow. The book is divided into two sections, "Physical Training" and "Mental Training" with a total of 18 chapters, each offering 5-20 major topics covering dozens of ways to help you be a better fighter.

I have had the pleasure of teaching the martial arts for many decades to students in my school, private students, police agencies, private security companies, mental health organizations, and various city bureaus. The slant in my personal training and teaching has always been toward surviving a real fight, therefore I can't help letting that prejudice slip through in this book. While I'm happy to report that the training tips I offer have worked for students in the harsh reality of violent encounters, I believe you will find that many of them will also help you in competition, or can be easily modified a little for the specific requirements of sport.

There is a method to my madness here, though it may appear at first glance to be a hodgepodge of concepts, principles and techniques for virtually all areas of the fighting arts. It would have been easy to write a book of 5000 ways to fight better, but it would have cost you as much as your car. So, because of space limitations, I have limited the ways to those that I have found especially valuable in my training, competing and my job as a police officer. I have also included a few that were given to me specifically for this book by instructors I hold in high regard because of their knowledge, ability and their track record of success in real-world confrontations. I have also tried to give credit here for information that I have gotten from martial artists I've talked with over the years, trained with or read about in books and magazines. I'm sorry if I've left anyone out, but having been punched and kicked in the head since 1965, my memory isn't what it use to be.

A word on the writing

While women make up a significant percentage of martial arts students, for ease of writing, I have used "he" instead of the awkward "he/she" and "him/her." I have also used the word "karate" as a generic term and hope I'm not offending readers involved in the many other kick/punch fighting arts.

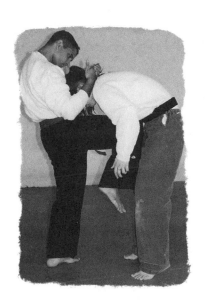

PART ONE

PHYSICAL TRAINING

10 ways

to Train Alone

I love to train by myself and have always encouraged my students to train alone at least once a week. Solo training is a time when you can do whatever *you* want to do. No one is telling you to work on a punching drill when you really want to polish your roundhouse kick, and no one is telling you to spar when you have yet to heal from your last session. Solo training is your time to train as hard or as easy as you like, for as long as you like. You can do it in your underwear while watching *The Brady Bunch* reruns on the tube, or do it in the basement to burn off frustration after a squabble with a family member. You get to choose the time, you get to choose the place and you get to work on anything you want.

One of the complaints I've often heard from students is that training alone is boring. How can that be? If you go into your solo training with the right mind set, that is, you picture before you an ugly, salivating beast of a human being who wants to rip your head off, how can your desperate fight for survival be boring?

Use your imagination when you train alone, just as you did when you played by yourself as a child. Make the imaginary attacker your boss, ex-spouse, the guy who cut you off on the freeway, the punks who threw trash in your yard, or that mean school teacher with the bony fingers. While this might seem a little sick, psychologists say it's actually a healthy (and legal) way to let off steam. It doesn't matter who you see in your mind's eye, as long as the image brings out your warrior spirit to enable you to train intensely and get a good workout.

Here are 10 ways to make your solo training interesting, challenging and make you a better fighter.

1. SHADOWBOXING

I have always felt that students who don't incorporate shadowboxing in their training are missing a valuable aid to their growth. As the name implies, shadowboxing involves your moving about the room punching, kicking and blocking an imaginary opponent who is throwing punches and kicks back at you. Here are just a few of the things you get from it.

Cardiovascular Benefits

If you want to improve your wind for sparring, then spar. Don't jog, climb the stair master, or swim laps down at the creek. Instead, work to develop your cardiovascular system doing the very thing you want aerobic conditioning for - in this case, to be able to spar without getting weak in the legs and blue in the face.

To get in good cardio condition, you need to shadowbox for at least 20 minutes two or three times a week with your heart rate sustained at about 75 to 80 percent of your maximum. Here is how you determine your maximum heart rate and then your training heart rate.

Males, take the number 220 and females take the number 226 and subtract your age. The difference is your maximum heart rate. Multiply this by the percentage you want to train at and that will give you the heart rate you need to maintain throughout your shadowboxing session. Here is how it looks if you are a 20-year-old male.

$220 - 20 = 200 \times .75 = 150$ beats a minute

If this male is out of shape, he should reduce his training percentage of his maximum heart rate to 60 percent and then progressively increase it as his aerobic condition improves. Even when you are in good shape, it's never a good idea to sustain a rate or 85 percent of higher.

Your pulse sites are at your wrist and the side of your neck. Stop sparring and check one of them for six seconds and then resume sparring. Multiply the number of beats you felt by 10. If you felt 15 beats, 15 multiplied by 10 is 150 beats per minute. If you are 20 years old, you are right on target. If you counted 10 beats, you need to pick up the pace, but if you counted 20, you need to slow down.

Improve your Timing with Music

Select music that has a pronounced rhythm and then block, kick and punch to its beat. You will find yourself moving about rhythmically and launching your techniques reflexively to the beat as if responding to openings and attacks with a real opponent. A nice side benefit is that music has a way of camouflaging your fatigue, enabling you to train longer and harder. But watch out, when the sounds stop, fatigue will hit you like a truck.

To find your pulse, use your fingers to press at the hollow between your ear and jaw, or along your wrist

Coordinating Footwork with Combinations

It's one thing standing before a mirror and throwing your combinations, and it's quite another shadowboxing combinations as you move about the room without entangling your feet. The latter provides you with the opportunity to launch your combinations from constant motion as you move forward, backward, sideways, bob and weave.

You Always get to Win

You always come out on top when you shadowbox an invisible opponent (unless you are a masochist and deliberately lose). All your techniques get to the target without being blocked, you are always successful at blocking your opponent's kicks and punches, and your match always ends with you as the victor. Savor the moment as few wins in life are this easy.

2. ENVIRONMENTAL TRAINING

As a former police officer who has been in dozens of physical force situations, I can tell you that not one of them ever took place in a nice, wide-open space or on mats like those in your martial arts school. I've fought people on roof tops, on the edge of a dock over a river, in a slimy skid row bathroom, on stairways, inside of a car engulfed in flames, and many other places I had never thought of when I was learning my techniques.

Training in different environments is a fun and beneficial way to learn more about your favorite moves. Consider conducting your solo training in the following places around your house.

Stairs

It's a whole different world trying to defend yourself on 12-inch wide steps as opposed to a wide-open floor. Do your rep practice and shadow boxing while moving up and down a set of stairs, while leaning against the wall with one foot on a high step and the other on a low one. Evaluate your favorite techniques as to what you can and can't do while trying to maintain your footing.

Cluttered Room

Practice your techniques in your cluttered basement or in your crowded attic. Don't move anything out of the way. Move around those boxes, kick over that stack of tires, jump over that collection of newspapers and move around that pile of unwashed clothes. If barefoot, look out for mousetraps.

Small Room

I've fought people in restroom stalls, clothes closets, and phone booths. Once I thrashed around with a man in that narrow space between a bedroom wall and the bed, on which his wife laid with a knife protruding from her throat. You quickly realize that you can't do your techniques in these places the same way you do them in your school. Train in a small room, like your bathroom or pantry, to learn more about your punches and kicks.

* See *Training Outdoors, #9* for one more fun and beneficial way to train in the environment.

3. REPS

Everyone in karate is looking for *the* secret that will make them faster, stronger and an overall better fighter. Well, there is something that will do it, but it's not a secret.

It's repetitions, lots and lots of reps. If you are a disciplined hard trainer, you already know this. But if you are one of those students who is under the impression that doing a new technique a half dozen times is all that is needed, here is a revelation: You need to do lots more.

The concept is simple: The more times you *correctly* repeat your kicks, punches and kata, the better you will be at them. The trick, however, is to make the reps interesting. The way I practiced when I began in the 1960's - sitting in horse stance and executing punch after punch after punch - just doesn't get it in the new millennium. You still need to do reps, but there are other ways to do them that are enjoyable and more beneficial. Here are three ways.

1000 Punches

This is a fun drill (well, maybe not *too* fun) that not only improves your punches when done twice weekly for four weeks, but also improves your mental fortitude and leaves you with a feeling of accomplishment. First break the 1000 punches into sets.

Here is one example. If you don't like this break down, create your own. You might want to do them all in just five sets or break them into 20 sets. It doesn't matter how you do them and how many reps you do in each set as long as you get in the 1000.

METHOD	SETS	REPS
Lead leg lunge	50 reps each side	100 reps
On one knee	50 reps each side	100 reps
Moving backwards	50 reps each side	100 reps
On stairs	50 reps each side	100 reps
Horse stance	50 reps each arm	100 reps
Sitting in a chair	50 reps each arm	100 reps
Combination roundhouse kick and punch	50 reps each side	100 reps
Backfist and punch	50 reps each side	100 reps
Lunge step and double punch with same arm	50 double punches each side	200 reps
		TOTAL: 1000 reps

Rep training is one of the most important training concepts in karate. I discuss it many more times throughout this book.

4. WORK WEAK TECHNIQUES

Let's say you have one lousy technique. Okay, you have lots, but for our purposes here, let's say you only have one and it's your sidekick. Your front, round and back kicks are looking good, but that sidekick goes out crooked, lands toes first, and then drops to the floor like a sack of spuds. You rarely use it because it's hard to execute, it looks bad, and it's, well, it's just a big, fat embarrassment.

Since you hate executing the kick in public, do it when you train alone in the privacy of your own home. First, make sure that you completely understand the mechanics of how the sidekick is executed. To refresh your memory, talk to your instructor about it, find a book or magazine that illustrates the sidekick step-by-step, or ask a fellow student who has a particularly good one. Once you are clear on the how-to-do process, it's time to sweat.

Your plan is to spend two or three days a week working on the kick at home. Here is your itinerary.

• Do inside leg, groin and hip stretches so that your sidekick travels smoothly and effortlessly.

• Do three sets of 10-15 reps of only the chamber portion of the kick to build strength in the pre-launch stage. Hold for one to two seconds at its highest point.

• Perform 10 -15 reps of the kick in slow motion to strengthen all the muscles involved in its delivery.

• Work on various ways to close the distance to get to the target. Do one to two sets of 10 reps of each method.

• Once you feel you have the motion of the kick perfected, add three sets of 10 reps of fast kicking.

It's important that you don't progress to fast reps until you can perform the kick flawlessly. I know you will be anxious to do them fast, but control yourself until you are absolutely ready. When your form is flawless, your speed will develop seemingly overnight.

The final stage is for you to prepare to get lots of compliments from your teacher and fellow students. Be humble and say something like, "Aw, shucks. Thank yuh, thank yuh."

5. KARATE BETWEEN WEIGHTS SETS

I try to use every second I'm in the weight gym. I'm not one who likes to sit around between sets of curls (okay, maybe I do a little posing in the mirror), but I prefer to fill the "rest" period with those karate movements I don't normally get to work on during class time. I'm not only benefitting from some extra martial arts training, but I'm getting in some aerobic work since I'm constantly moving without a rest period.

Here are some techniques I do between weight sets and between weight exercises to get a little free karate training in. Try these or replace them with whatever you need to work on.

Exercise	In between the sets
Bench press 4 sets	Chambered leg lifts as if I were going to throw a kick 4 sets, 15 reps
Curls 4 sets	Bob and weave as if evading a head punch 4 sets, 45 seconds
Triceps press 4 sets	Practice various forms of footwork for gap closing 4 sets, 15 reps
Shoulder press 4 sets	Practice getting up from the floor fast 4 sets, 15 reps

There are others, but you get the idea. I try to incorporate fighting techniques that are rather obscure, but are nonetheless important.

6. HEAVY BAG

Here is a way to work on the heavy bag by yourself that builds power, endurance and lets you know which techniques need additional work.

Begin by placing a clock where you can see the second hand. Your objective is to strike the bag 60 times for 60 seconds, that's one per second for those of you who are as bad at math as I am. No matter what technique you throw - punch, kick, head butt, shoulder ram - do it hard. Work to ensure that your form is perfect: your hips are rotating, your opposite hand is snapping back, your balance is solid, and your energy is going into the bag.

When you are ready, maybe in a week or two, increase the time to two minutes and throw 120 hard techniques, one for each second. Be sure to move around as if you were sparring: bobbing, weaving, shuffling and sliding. Throw singles and combinations, counting each hit on the bag as one.

You may have to stay at the two-minute count for two or more weeks until you are in shape to progress. This is quite taxing so progress wisely. When you are ready, add another one-minute set. Now you are doing one, two-minute set, hitting the bag 120 times, resting for a minute, and then hitting the bag 60 times for another minute.

For the next stage, and let me warn you again to progress slowly, add one more minute to the second round, which will increase your hits for that round to 120. Now it looks like this.

Set 1: two minutes, 120 hits

Rest: for a minute

Set 2: two minutes, 120 hits

There are a couple of ways you can increase at this point. You can continue to progressively add one and two minute sets until you work up to a 20-minute cardiovascular workout. Or, if you just want to do this exercise for only two, two-minute sets, but you want to increase your output, you can add more hits per minute. World Champion kickboxer Kathy Long likes to throw 200 - 300 hits per two-minute session, and she always strives to make each hit hard, fast and accurate.

It's easy to get the pulse up to 90 percent of maximum heart rate with this routine. Since most trainers recommend 75 - 85 percent, 90 percent is too high, so don't stay at that extreme too long. Progress slowly with this workout, especially if you are out of shape cardiovascularly.

7. TRAIN TO YOUR FAVORITE MUSIC

I mentioned earlier that it's fun and beneficial to shadowbox to music. Here is another way you can train to the tunes.

Whether it's rock music, Beethoven, Barry Manilow (sheesh!), country western, or whatever, your favorite music touches your spirit and energizes your muscles. This is your time, your solo workout, so choose whatever sparks your plug.

I like powerful Asian music. I've been to the Orient a few times and certain music transports me to that place where martial arts basically began. If I'm listening to Japanese music, I let my wild imagination conjure an image of a small, vulnerable village nesting at the base of Mt. Fuji. The people there have come to me, a highly-trained samurai, and asked that I give them protection against marauding bandits in the area (I know this is sort of weird, but hey, I don't poke fun at your fantasies). I get a tremendous charge as I train with that music in my ears and that image in my mind, all of which psyches my brain and adds speed and power to my movements.

For an easy workout, choose soft, gentle music. Maybe you want to polish your kicking and punching form by doing the movements slowly and gracefully, sort of tai chi-like. This can make for a relaxing workout that will calm your spirit and mellow your psyche.

If you want a cardio workout to improve your endurance, choose music that gets you moving, that makes you want to rock and roll with punches and kicks. Turn up the volume of a tune that has a pronounced beat and just go crazy. This is fun and will energize you even on those days when you are feeling tired. It improves your endurance and flow and, when you train to hit on each pronounced beat, your rhythm and timing will improve, too.

Experiment with music and see how it effects you mentally, physically and spiritually.

8. TRAIN WHILE WATCHING THE TUBE

There are some areas in your karate training where you need to train with intense concentration, such as when you are polishing a complicated kata movement or an intricate fighting combination. But there are also things you can do while training by yourself that don't require a lot of concentration. For these exercises, it's okay to do them while watching your favorite TV program.

Stretching

Turn on MTV, drop down on the floor and do a few of your favorite stretches. You can listen to the music, give an occasional glance at the screen and improve your flexibility.

Reflexes

Turn on a talky program, such as the evening news, and begin shuffling around on the balls of your feet. Select two or three common words, such as *the, a*, and *is* and listen for the newsperson to say them as you move about. When you hear your selected word, explode with a kick or punch. While this is an audio exercise, it nonetheless conditions your reflexes to react.

Visually, try punching or kicking each time the scene changes or someone on the screen does a particular action. For example, throw a technique every time the news anchor blinks or looks down at his papers, or every time a field reporter adjusts his hand-held microphone. The idea is to create a reflexive response to a visual stimulus. While the stimulus in this case is harmless, the benefit overlaps to stimuli that is not harmless, such as your opponent's surprise punch.

For an extra hard TV workout, throw punches and kicks in response to both visual and audio stimuli. Throw a technique every time you see that news person blink, say "a," look down at his papers, say "the," adjust his hand-held microphone, and say "is." Do this for 15 minutes and your reflexes will be so on edge that you will need to meditate afterwards just to relax.

9. TRAIN OUTDOORS

This goes along with "Environmental Training," but it's so special I wanted to list it separately. Training outdoors is a wonderful way to get fresh air, a little sun and to experience a whole different feel to your usual workout.

I have had some incredible solo outdoor workouts. I've done kata in a forest clearing in Kyoto, Japan, and I've trained in the middle of a dirt road in Vietnam's countryside. I've practiced karate reps on the beach at sundown, and tai chi at sunrise. I've practiced slow punching combinations during a snowfall and worked my kata in the rain. I've worked out in parks, in backyards, in driveways and on street corners. I even attempted to sit in horse stance and do a few punches during a hurricane in Florida, but that ended when I was sent rolling painfully along the ground.

I saw lots of examples of solo training outdoors in the Orient. I watched people doing kung fu forms along the banks of the Saigon River and, from my hotel window in Seoul, Korea, I watched a taekwondo man practicing kicks on the roof of a 25-story high-rise. In Hong Kong and China, I saw countless people training by themselves wherever there was a little space, like the guy working out on a six-foot wide traffic medium on a busy Hong Kong street.

There is something about training by yourself outdoors that lifts your spirit and leaves you with a sense of having experienced something special. Give it a try, you'll like it.

10. TRAINING IN WATER

I'm not talking about punching and kicking in the shower; those little drops don't offer much in the way of resistance. But when you are submerged in a body of water up to your neck, you get resistance throughout the entire range of your technique.

If you haven't trained in water before, take it easy at first and build up to a hard workout. Once I was feeling fat and sluggish on vacation, so I decided to train for an hour in the ocean, doing dozens of punches, kicks, blocks and lunges. It was a dumb decision. I was soooo sore that I had to cancel a hike the next day, and I had a sore hip and knee for a week. Start out slowly and progress slowly.

The beauty of training in the water is that it provides constant resistance. With many barbell and dumbbell exercises, gravity helps you do part of the movement, which reduces the resistance you want. When you curl a barbell, gravity takes over about 3/4 of the way into the upward arc, which causes the bar to drop the rest of the way to your shoulder. This does not happen in the water. For example, consider doing an uppercut punch, a motion similar to the curl. When you execute the movement under water, don't stop the punch where you normally would, but continue pushing your fist up and into a big arc until it's 2 or 3 inches from your shoulder, just as you would curl a barbell. Since gravity has little effect under water, the resistance remains constant throughout the movement.

Here is a good underwater workout to exercise your arms and legs in all the basic directions. To stimulate the fast-twitch muscles, the ones that make your movements fast and explosive, do the following movements as fast as you can. But, and this is a big but, do so only after you have done a set or two at slow to medium speed to thoroughly warm up your muscles and joints.

Reverse punches	3 sets, 10 reps
Backfists	3 sets, 10 reps
Uppercuts	3 sets, 10 reps
Roundhouse punches	3 sets, 10 reps
Backhand blocks	3 sets, 10 reps
Palm sweep blocks	3 sets, 10 reps

Front kicks	3 sets, 10 reps
Sidekicks	3 sets, 10 reps
Roundhouse kicks	3 sets, 10 reps
Back kicks	3 sets, 10 reps

For sure there are many other techniques you can do, but this is a good starter workout because it stimulates your foundation techniques in all basic directions of force.

Let's say you feel strong in the basics, but you want to train a couple of other techniques that you consider weak. Working them once or twice in the constant-resistance environment of water will bring them up to speed in a month.

By the way, skinny-dip training is another option.

to Improve your Hand Techniques

Kicking stylists will probably disagree, but real fights involve mostly hand techniques. While my approach to training has always been 50 percent punches/50 percent kicks, I've used my feet only a few times in my many physical confrontations as a police officer. Most often, I had my hands on the guy when the fight exploded, so I was at a range that was too close to get off a kick.

I'm definitely not saying that kicks are unimportant. When I did use them, they worked like a charm (one time in a Saigon bar, I sidekicked a guy coming at me with a barstool. He flew backwards across the room, crashed through a door and landed on his back out in the kitchen. He started to come back at me, but changed his mind and ran out the back door). But in my experience, and in the experience of others who have survived lots of real-life encounters, hand techniques are used the most often.

Here are 10 ways to make your fists fast and powerful.

1. SHOULDERS

Far too many students raise their shoulders when they punch, in particular, when reverse punching. Sometimes they look down their extended arm as if looking down a rifle barrel at a turkey shoot. Lifting the shoulders at the completion of the reverse punch weakens its power because it eliminates the involvement of the upper back muscles and the latisimus dorsi muscles, commonly referred to as the lats.

Try this test. Extend your reverse punch with your shoulder down and feel your lat muscle just below and to the outside of your armpit. With your shoulder down, your lat muscle is flexed because it's contributing to the punch. Now, with your hand still on your flexed lat, raise your shoulder. It's no longer flexed, is it? When your shoulder is hunched it becomes the weak link in your power chain because it eliminates the involvement of your major back muscle.

An Exception to the Rule

But are there occasions when you can raise your shoulders when punching? Mike Ferguson, a Muay Thai fighter based in Canada, says there are some techniques that require it.

"While I shadowbox," Ferguson says, "I try to stretch and loosen my shoulders by throwing hooks and uppercuts, allowing my shoulders so much room to move. My shoulders generally pop up and slap my jaw a little. This 'jaw slapping' happens when you get enough rotation and you are really relaxed. It's a good sign that you are loose."

As a Muay Thai fighter, Ferguson uses a stance similar to boxer's. "My stance is a little high and I lift my shoulders so my hands can cover my face better. As far as the delivery of straight punches, I don't change the position of my shoulders. When I have my guard up by my temples, my shoulders are up, and when I throw a punch, my shoulder slaps my face. My fist comes right from my jaw. If my shoulders are down all the way, and I'm relaxed, I throw the punch from my chest, but still my shoulder touches my chin a little."

While Muay Thai fighters raise their shoulders for a few of their punches and therefore negate some involvement of their upper back muscles, they make up for the loss by rotating their shoulders and waist further than do most karate styles (more in a moment why you should incorporate this rotation).

Mike Ferguson says that having relaxed shoulders is important for speed and power. "You want to keep your shoulders relaxed because you want to be really loose. If your shoulders are all tight, chances are you will be using your arms to punch instead of your whole body. When doing a lot of punches, tight shoulders will actually slow you down, while relaxed shoulders improve your snap. Most importantly, you want to keep your shoulders relaxed so you don't lose power.

2. ROTATING YOUR BODY

I can still remember my first instructor telling the class of the importance of snapping the hips forward when throwing a reverse punch. "You will increase your power by 80 percent," he told us. I don't know if he just grabbed that percentage out of the air to make his statement sound more official, but for sure, rotating the hips adds tremendous power to some hand techniques.

Rotating While Exercising in Horse Stance

Let's consider the reverse punch. Hopefully, you understand that sitting in a deep horse stance and punching straight ahead from the hip is just an exercise. You would never - heavens forbid - ever do that in a real fight. As an exercise, it serves as a pretty good way to simultaneously strengthen the legs while working the involved punching muscles in the arm, chest, back and shoulders. However, many styles, especially the more rigid traditionalists, don't rotate their hips or turn their shoulders when punching in horse stance. In fact, many traditionalists consider it blasphemy.

I still remember my kong su instructor shouting at the class, as we sat low and pounded out rep after rep, "Stop turning your shoulders! Keep them square to the front! Don't turn your hips! Keep them motionless!" I never questioned this back then when I was a young neophyte, though I wish now I would have.

Today in my school, we occasionally do the classic-horse stance punching exercise, but with a twist (pun intended). We get low in the stance, hold our arms high, fists just below the jaw line, and thrust our punch forward as we snap the other fist back to our ear. The big difference is that we rotate our upper body as we punch, including the shoulders. You can turn the hip with the punch just a tad, but the emphasis is on rotating the upper body.

Punching in this fashion while exercising in horse stance keeps the concept of rotation alive in your mind. Why ingrain in your subconscious a rigid way of punching in horse stance, but then use hip snap and shoulder rotation when punching in your fighting stance? Always remember that how you train is how you perform for real. Secondly, when you punch rigidly in horse stance, you don't stimulate the muscles that rotate your shoulders and waist. Every supplemental exercise you do should work the same muscles you are going to use when throwing a technique from your fighting stance.

Incorrect

While a good exercise, one problem with rigid horse-stance punching is that it conditions   the mind not to sink the punch.

Correct

However, slightly rotating the waist and shoulders trains the mind to sink the punch deeper, and exercises the muscles involved in the extension.

Incorrect

Rigid punching in your forward stance limits your power potential and your reach.

Correct

Without stepping, rotate your hips, waist & shoulders to increase impact and reach. Notice the line on the wall and how far the puncher extends without taking a step.

Rotating in your Fighting Stance

The classic reverse punch is usually done by extending the arm in conjunction or slightly before the rotation of the hips. This is fine. But many styles stop the rotation when both shoulders form a straight line, a position sometimes referred to as "flush to the front." This is okay if that is where your target mandates that you stop your rotation, but too many karate students *always* stop at this point. This is unfortunate, because when you have the option of rotating your hips and shoulders further, but don't take it, you greatly reduce your power and penetration capability.

How far should you twist? As much as 45 degrees beyond flush to the front. When throwing a right reverse punch, continue twisting your shoulders until your chest is angled to your left at a 45-degree angle.

Try this experiment. Face a wall and extend your right punching arm until your chest and shoulders are parallel to it and your fist is touching. Keep your arm up as you scoot your feet back until your fist is about 12-15 inches away from the wall. This is where a fighter's punch would stop who does not rotate his shoulders and hips. Now, without moving your feet, rotate your shoulders, waist and hips about 45 degrees to the left. Hey! Your fist is now resting against the wall and you didn't take a step. This simple illustration proves the reach potential gained when rotating the body in the reverse punch.

To test the dramatic penetration power of the rotation, try it on the heavy bag. First hit it with a punch with your shoulders flush to the front and then again with a hip, waist and shoulder rotation 45 degrees to the side.

3. TRICKY-KNEE PUNCH

No, this doesn't have anything to do with a bad knee or punching at the knee; it's just my way of being linguistically clever. It does, however, involve doing a quick bend of your lead knee to get a little closer to your opponent and hitting him just a little harder. This is a great trick to create an illusion that you are further away from your opponent than he thinks you are. Assume your fighting stance but position your feet a couple inches closer together than you normally do. To make him think you need glasses, throw a reverse punch that misses him by several inches. Throw another and twist your upper body just a little to show him that you are really trying. Ideally, he becomes lulled into a comfort zone because he thinks you are too far away to be dangerous (hee, hee, snicker).

The third time you punch (the third being the charm), bend both knees deeper, lean your upper body slightly forward and engage that shoulder and body twist we just discussed in #2. Tuh duh! Without taking a step, you increased your reach by more than 12 inches and punched a hole in his chest.

You can do this with your backfist, too; the only difference is that you rotate your upper body away as your arm extends and your knees bends. Throw out a couple strikes that miss your opponent by a mile, then sink your knees, lean in and whack him.

You can even combine your backfist and reverse punch. Set him up with one or two backfist misses, and then sink, extend and hit him with a quick one-two, a backfist and reverse punch combination.

Try not to laugh too hard at his look of surprise.

4. BOXER'S JAB

The jab may have originated with the "sweet science" of boxing, but karate people are free to use it too, though few do. I'm not talking about traditional karate's straight punch, which is about as sneaky as an out-of-control Mac truck with a stuck horn. Yes, the karate straight punch can be extremely powerful, but it's harder to sneak in than is the more versatile, easy-to-deliver and disarming boxer's jab.

The jab is most often delivered from a high stance, a boxer's stance, a position that allows your footwork to be fluid, light and highly mobile. It's a stance that makes for easy and quick movement in and out of range, which allows for more opportunities to set up your opponent.

This technique is especially popular in those styles that are reality based, although not too many years ago there were only a few karate fighters who knew how to defend against it. The first time I tried the jab against karate people outside of my school, it was like shooting ducks in a barrel. Each time I popped one, my opponents would flinch as if startled, and only a few of them blocked it, or even tried. Today, however, more fighters are familiar with the jab, and the only people who have problems with it now are those who don't include it in their personal arsenal or practice it in their style.

Historically Speaking

Just as many kung fu systems were created from watching animals, birds and even insects fight, early boxing most likely copied the way cats and bears slap and cuff their enemies. Historical boxing records show that before the jab came along, early fighters relied on swinging and hooking their blows. As boxing evolved, straight hitting was discovered and fighters found they could hit faster and more accurately with straight shots than with circular ones. They also found they could better maintain their balance, since it was safer to snap their punches straight out and back than it was to make over committed swings.

How to Jab

Let's take a look at the mechanics of the jab and see how using your hips is so important to delivering a fast and powerful blow.

Assume a left leg forward fighting stance with your hands up near your head. As your left   fist travels forward, turn your left shoulder and left hip no more than a quarter turn to your right until your arm is fully extended. If you turn so far that your entire left side is toward your opponent, as if drawing a bow to launch an arrow, you have gone too far. More is not better.

Technique: Jab

Assume your on-guard stance and snap your left arm straight out making sure to keep your elbow pointing downward. Rotate your upperbody about a 1/4 to the right. Snap it back on the same path.

Don't let your right arm hang down like a dead grape on a vine. When you launch your left jab, snap your right arm back to a place near your chin. Though this may be a boxer's jab, the karate principle still holds that for every action there is an opposite action. Snap your right hand back fast, and watch your jab go out even faster.

Your jabbing fist rotates until your palm is facing the floor at the point of impact. Some fighters hit with their thumb side up and with their fist turned downward slightly to make impact with their index and middle knuckles. You might want to experiment with this to see how you like it.

With either method, your arm travels in a straight line and strikes *through* the target, not *at* the target. If you are punching a guy in the neck (a safer target for your fist than his bony old chin), think of punching all the way through his Adam's apple to his back collar. It's the same thinking process for breaking a brick: You don't just hit the top of the brick, but you think all the way through.

The jab is a light and easy movement. But if you tense your shoulder, fist and arm prior to hitting, it will be stiff and slow. Practice the jab until it becomes a natural, almost casual movement. Experiment with lifting the shoulders as the Muay Thai fighter suggests on page 32, #1, "Shoulders" to see if you like that method. Practice hitting the air, hitting a heavy bag, a handheld pad, and a training partner's open palm. Then work your jab into your sparring. Your ultimate goal is to have a jab that is quick and powerful without apparent effort. Here are a few ways to use it.

Jab to Make your Opponent Nervous

As you move around stalking each other, keep popping jabs at your opponent's face. It doesn't matter whether you jab in an attempt to hit, or jab just to make your opponent flinch. Your objective is to keep him nervous and thinking about defense rather than thinking about attacking you.

To Disrupt your Opponent's Setpoint

Use the jab every time he sets himself to throw a technique at you. As the two of you spar, you see him get set to launch a punch. To disrupt his plan, lunge forward with your lead foot and snap a quick jab into his face.

Strategy Tip: Jab to Disrupt your Opponent

While sparring, you detect your opponent setting up an inverted punch.

You disrupt this with a quick jab to the side of his face and . . .

take advantage of his nicely exposed Adam's apple and punch it.

Jab to Set up your Opponent

This technique works especially well with the high/low and broken rhythm principle. Gary Sussman, my senior student and a 3rd-degree black belt who has been with me since 1982, loves to combine high/low with broken rhythm. "I like to jab high and then kick low," he says. "First, I'll jab at my opponent's face and let him block it. Then I'll jab at his face a second time, and again I let him block it. My third jab is a fake that goes out only enough to make him commit his block. When he does, I slam a kick into his groin or against his knee. The concept is simple: I set a rhythm with the jabs and then I break it."

Jabbing the Body

Not a lot of fighters jab to their opponent's body, but I have seen guys get hit there and crumple to the ground unable to continue fighting. Here is how to do it with power.

Boxers believe that the jabber's body should be behind the jab (as shown at right) whether it's to a high target or a mid level one. To jab hard to a low target, you need to lower your body so that your left shoulder is at a level with your opponent's solar plexus. Bend your lead leg slightly and your rear leg a little more as you rotate your shoulders, and drive your fist into your opponent's gut. Be sure to snap your other hand back to the side of your head. Since being low and close to your opponent is not a desirable place to loiter, especially if your jab didn't hurt him, follow up with additional techniques or scoot yourself out of there.

Add the jab to your repertoire and you will be happily surprised at how well it works - though not half as surprised as your opponent.

5. HOOK PUNCHES

The hook punch is another hand technique rarely found in karate styles. This is an unfortunate omission, since it's a devastating blow that can easily drop a street attacker. In point fighting competition, however, you might find it difficult to get the judges to call it since it's harder to see than the more obvious reverse punch. Additionally, because it's rarely seen in point competition, you might run into judges who won't count it as a point no matter how accurately or obviously it's thrown.

There are two kinds of hook punches: the lead and the rear. Both require considerable practice to perfect, but are well worth the effort. They can be sneaky and get into openings that other hand techniques can't, and they can be extremely powerful when executed with all the correct body mechanics.

Front Hook

Assume your fighting position with your left side forward, arms in an on-guard position and your front heal slightly off the floor. Some fighters like to hit with their palm facing downward, others prefer their palm facing back toward them. No matter which method you like, be sure to make contact with your two, large knuckles.

Think 90. Keep your punching arm bent about 90 degrees as you rotate your hip and foot in the direction of your punch. Your front foot twists 90 degrees to the right until your toes are pointing to your right side, as you simultaneously twist your hips about 90 degrees in the same direction. Your rear foot twists the same way, but only about 70 degrees. Under the stress of a real fight, you may not twist your lead foot all the way to 90 degrees, but your hips should twist as far as possible to maximize the impact of your punch. When practicing in the air, stop your left hook punch when it's even with your right side, and simultaneously snap your right fist back to your right ear.

It's all these factors working together that provides power to the hook.

Technique: Front Hook

Move to his outside as you block his straight punch.

You can easily pop him with a lad hook. Be sure to twist your front foot, hips and upper body to increase the impact of your punch.

Rear Hook

The big difference with the rear hook is that you are unable to twist your feet and hips to the degree that you can when hooking with your lead. It's still a deadly blow because it's traveling a greater distance to the target that the front hand. Be sure to snap your other hand back to your ear for greater hooking power.

Many trainers don't recommend either the front or rear hook as a lead technique unless you have exceptional speed.

Here are a few circumstances in which a hook works like a charm.

• Attack with a reverse punch to the opponent's middle and follow with a lead hook to the side of his neck. This works especially well in the street when the guy bends forward from the impact of the reverse punch, thus bringing his head down right there in front of you almost begging to be punched.

• The attacker is in an opposite stance and jabs at you. Slip to his outside and throw a lead hook around his guard and into his neck or ear.

• Your opponent drops his hands when he is within range. Ram a front hook punch into his ear.

• Your opponent throws a reverse punch that you sidestep and block. Throw a hard rear hook into his middle.

I encourage you to work your hook punches on the heavy bag to see if your blows are landing properly. Don't start out slamming it like a mad man because the bag may show you the errors of your ways by spraining your wrist (been there, done that). The heavy bag is a great teacher and it will tell you faster than any observer whether you are holding your hands correctly. Take it easy at first, and work your way up to harder blows.

Boxers love hook punches for a good reason: They inflict pain.

6. USING DOUBLE HAND PADS

If you don't use hand pads in your training, you should. There are many great exercises and drills you can do with them, and even more if you have a creative imagination.

Instructor Daniel Alix uses them to not only improve punching but to coordinate footwork as well. Here is one of his drills that is fun and beneficial. We tried it in my school after he sent it to me, and everyone saw a marked improvement in their hand skill by the end of the first training session.

"The instructor holds up two hand pads," Alix says, "both high, or one high and one low, while you practice simple combinations like high jab and low punch or a high hook and a low punch. After you get good at it, your instructor can wear body-armor so you can throw kicks at him along with your punches on the pads.

"After throwing several combinations, the instructor adds to the exercise by backing up, slowly at first and then faster and faster as you get proficient at pursuing. This gives you a chance to learn how to attack with multiple punches while advancing forward using whatever footwork you want. If you get care-less about how you move and attack with your hands, your instructor should throw mock punches or kicks at you to help you get back on track."

Alix says the next step is for the instructor to move toward you. "He either walks or he throws kicks at you, while you back up and hit the pads with com-binations. It's important that the instructor be the one to control the pace by forcing you to retreat faster and faster as your skill progresses. The instructor can also use walls and corners to try to trap you.

"Another way is to have the instructor wear a boxing glove on one hand, and a focus target on the other. He keeps you on your toes by jabbing with his gloved hand and throwing kicks. As before, he begins by standing in one place. When you are proficient at that level, he advances to moving backward, and when you are responding well with that, he moves toward you. In all stages, he keeps moving the pad around and tossing out the occasional punch and kick. Your job is to avoid getting hit while you attack the moving target."

This a great exercise that will quickly improve your ability to incorporate your footwork, blocking, evading, and attacking while on the move.

7. GOOFY BAG

Another name for this training device could easily be "The Humbler" since it can make you feel like an idiot if you have never trained on it, or have laid off of it for a few months. What gives the bag its goofy quality is that it's suspended in the air by an elastic cord attached to its top and another to its bottom. A mere tap sends it into a mad frenzy of bobbing, twirling and erratic spinning. It's this quality that makes it a good training device.

While martial artists spend an inordinate amount of time working drills that target their opponent's head, it's actually not that easy to hit. A fighter with even a little training, or a fighter with no training but a lot of instinct, can easily move his head to avoid being struck. One of the two reasons police agencies don't hit suspects in the head with their police batons is because most people expect to be struck there, so they are on guard against it. The second reason is that usually the head bleeds like a gaffed fish, even from a minor blow. When a photographer captures the moment of bloody impact for the evening news, it's not good for public relations, no matter how lowly or deserving the criminal.

The goofiness of this bag makes for an excellent training tool that increases your ability to punch with accuracy. Even the slightest tap will send it jerking and writhing all over the place. But once you get proficient at hitting it, your ability to hit a human head will increase tenfold. And it doesn't take long to develop proficiency. In fact, you will experience a marked improvement in as little as 30 minutes.

Your First Workout

Assume your fighting stance and stand before the bag. Slam a hard backfist into it and watch it fly away and, quick as a wink, snap back and smash you in the face. When you feel a geyser of blood erupt from your nose, cover it with a towel and end your workout.

Your Second Workout

Wiser from your first training session, you are respectful of the goofy bag and all the surprises of which it's capable. You have learned that it's not about hitting hard, but rather hitting with accuracy. Hit it lightly this time and observe how it propels outward and how quickly it returns on its irregular path. Hit it again, and watch it shoot off in diagonal direction and then return quickly on a completely different trajectory, forcing you to lean out of the way. Smack it again, and watch it warp and shimmy and fling back at you from another direction. This time you are taken by surprise, and you slap at it like a kindergartner.

This is all part of the learning process. The more you do it, though, the better you get at it. You may not always be able to read how it's going to fly out and return, but you will learn to move about and hit it no matter how wobbly and erratic it comes back. In time, you will be dancing, bobbing, weaving, slipping and ducking as you assault it with jabs, backfists and straight punches.

With regular training on the bag, you will be better able to hit your opponent's moving head. Even if he is good at head evasion, he will never be as tricky as the goofy bag.

8. PUSH-UPS

The motion of the push-up is virtually the same as the jab, reverse punch and other straight-line-type punches. It makes sense then to incorporate lots of push-ups in your conditioning routine, and there is a large variety to use. One time I was teaching a class of 30 students, and as a way of ending the training session, I asked each person to lead the class in a different pushup variation for 10 reps. Not only did each student come up with a different one, we came up with an additional 10 variations for a total of 40. Here are a few:

* Hands spaced wide   * Hands spaced narrow
* One-arm   * On thumbs and index fingers
* On knuckles   * On the backs of your hands
(ouch) * On fingertips   * Fingers facing each other
* Do only bottom half   * Clap hands at top of pushup
* With thumbs and index fingers touching
* Begin on forearms and roll up onto hands
Use some or all of the above and feel free to add some of your own. They are all good for your punches.

Here is a variation I found recently that, although quite stressful on your joints, will greatly increase the explosiveness of your punches. If you have bad elbows, shoulders, back or arms, don't do this method. But if your parts are all in good working order, include them once a week in your workout. It's okay if you want to do other variations on other days of the week, but I wouldn't push it too hard. This method is so stressful that you risk overtraining if you do too many others.

Here is how it's done.

Push-up Jumps and Drops

Set up two six-inch-high platforms or cinder blocks, parallel with each other and about shoulder width apart. It's more comfortable if you place the blocks on a mat or some other kind of padding.

Begin by placing your hands on the blocks in the standard push-up position, and then drop your hands simultaneously between them and allow your chest to go all the way to the mat. Without hesitation, straighten your arms and explode upward until your hands are completely off the mat and back onto the blocks. Again without hesitation, drop your hands back down onto the mat, touch your chest and then thrust forcefully back up again.

This push-up method will definitely build explosiveness in your straight-line punches. Do three to four sets of four to six repetitions.

Let me warn you again to be careful as this is a risky exercise. But if you have no preexisting injuries and you do the exercise correctly, you will see a marked differences in your hand techniques in just a few weeks.

Place your hands on two cinder blocks that are a little wider than your shoulders.

Push off and drop to the ground . . .

. . . until your chest touches . . .

. . . and then forcefully explode back up and onto the blocks. Your reps should be done non-stop with explosive pushes.

49

9. STRENGTHENING YOUR ABS FOR BETTER PUNCHES

Let's take a look at how you can improve your hand techniques and at the same time develop a six-pack of abdominal muscles that will make 'em swoon at the beach. Now, aren't you glad you bought this book?

Your abdominal muscles are positioned at the center of your body (if yours are elsewhere get a hold of me and I'll write an article about you) and, when strengthened, they dramatically increase the power of your hand techniques, as well as your kicks. This is because a strong midsection is like a rocket booster for your moves. When you involve your abs in, say, your backfist, your ab power flows from your middle, up to your shoulders, down your arms and out your fist.

There are dozens of abdominal exercises floating around; if you don't know any you can find them in books, magazines and on exercise videos. The best book I have seen on the subject is one called *The Complete Book of Abs* by Kurt Brungardt, published by Villard Books.

The only stipulation I have to including an ab exercise in my routine is that it's safe. While most of the newer exercises are, there are still old ones being used that are potentially dangerous to your back. Case in point are those old sit-ups that require you to raise all the way up. Those are the kind my generation did in highschool and probably account for why so many baby boomers have back problems today. *The Complete Book of Abs* not only lists dozens of exercises, but also rates them as to how safe they are.

Choose ab exercises that work the lower abdominal area as well as the easy-to-develop   upper abs. In most exercises, it's important to press the small of your back into the floor so as to not strain or injure that area. If any exercise hurts your back - eliminate it. Don't keep doing it because you are a macho kind of guy. If you are a student, and one of your instructor's ab exercises hurts you, don't do it and tell him why. A back injury can affect your life forever. Besides, there are lots of other exercises you can do that won't hurt it.

Any exercise that requires you to raise your legs should be done with them bent slightly and with the small of your back pressed into the floor. This puts more stress on your abs as it removes it from your lower back.

How many reps should you do? As many as it takes. Sometimes when I'm lifting weights, I put a 25-pound barbell plate on my chest and I exhaust my muscles with only three sets of 15 reps of the basic crunch exercise. In class, however, we always burn out 200-300 reps of an assortment of crunches and leg lifts. As is the case with any exercise, I believe that variety is the key to keeping the muscles stimulated and your mind interested.

The Ab/Fist Connection

Here is how you incorporate your abs with your hand techniques. First, give this a try while you are sitting there in your chair reading this book. As hard as you can, tense your abs for just a fraction of a second, and then do it again a couple times to get a sense of how this makes your ab muscles feel. Remember that sensation, because that is exactly what you want to do as your fist hits its target.

Now, try it striking with your backfist against a heavy bag. Assume your stance and snap your backfist toward the bag with a lead-leg lunge. When your fist is about four inches away from impact, tense your abs as hard as you can. As you do so, exhale sharply while you mentally force energy from your ab muscles up your chest, along your arm and out your fist. That's it, pretty easy. But once you get this coordinated, you will see and feel at least a 25 percent improvement on the bag.

Do this with your jab, reverse punch, uppercut and all your other hand techniques. The stronger your abs, the harder you hit.

And if you watch your calories and reduce your body fat, you and your new abs will be the envy at the beach.

10. HAND TOUGHENING

Toughening the hands is a controversial subject that has been debated for years in the martial arts. Consider the following Q and A.

Q. Is it absolutely necessary to build thick callouses on your knuckles to have an effective punch?

A. No.

Q. Is it potentially dangerous?

A. It can be, especially when you injure the bones.

O. Is there a relatively safe way to build them?

A. Yes

Q. Are big, calloused knuckles impressive to look at?

A. Some people think so.

Q. Do they make for a harder hand strike?

A. Yes.

I've worked at toughening my knuckles off and on for all of my martial arts career. There have been times when they were thick with callousness and there have been times when I've stopped working them and the callouses diminished (maintaining them is a continuous process). One time while in Vietnam, a country where the people are quite aware of the martial arts and notice such things as calloused knuckles, a dozen Vietnamese people gathered around me after one of my brawls as a military policeman and stared at my hands as they talked excitedly among themselves about my knuckles. The only word I could understand them saying was "taekwondo," the primary martial art in Vietnam at the time.

Other than for cosmetic purposes, calloused knuckles, especially if they are thick and hard, add to the impact of your punch. One Chinese master, who strikes a metal plate 1000 times a day and has knuckles nearly as large as golf balls, says that hitting someone with his knuckles is like hitting them with a rock. He also says that he doesn't feel pain in his knuckles because he has long ago deadened the nerves in them.

Whether to toughen your knuckles or not is, of course, your decision. You may find that toughening them is a long and painful process that has no benefit other than impressing white belts. On the other hand, you may find that building them is beneficial to your punching. If you choose to do it, you should know that there is some risk involved, especially if you build them by repetitiously striking a hard object, like the aforementioned metal plate. When doing it that way, it's quite possible to cause irreversible damage to the nerves, so much so that you could spend the rest of your life walking around with a hand frozen in the shape of a claw.

There is, however, a way to put callouses on your knuckles by toughening the skin rather than damaging the bones. This may be a superficial way to build up the knuckles and not as effective as enlarging and toughening the bones, but it nonetheless puts a layer of protection on them. This is the way I have always done it and, when they are at their best, I can hit a hard object without feeling much pain.

Knuckle Push-ups

Do your push-ups on the large knuckles of your index and middle fingers. They are your primary striking points, and therefore the ones you want to toughen. Just doing push-ups on them won't toughen the skin much, so you need to twist your hand ever so slightly so that your knuckles rub into the floor. The keyword here is twist "slightly" because the weight on your knuckles is significant, and too much twisting will tear the skin, a not-so-fun moment in time that stings like the dickens. Start out doing these on a carpet, then progress to wood and then cement.

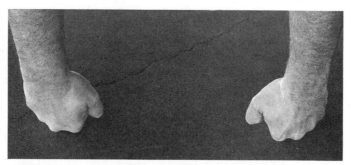

Make sure your weight is on your index and middle knuckles
and twist them ever so slightly in the up position.

Rub a Brick

Actually, you can rub your knuckles with a rock, a piece of wood, cement or anything else that has a rough surface. Place your two large knuckles on the object and rotate your hand back and forth in a vigorous rubbing motion. Don't get carried away and press too hard because you will tear the skin. As your skin grows tougher you can press progressively harder.

Punch a Canvas Bag

Modern-day heavy bags are usually made out of slick, smooth vinyl. These are excellent for developing power in your techniques, but they don't do much toward toughening the skin over your knuckles. Canvas-covered heavy bags, however, work wonderfully. They are hard to find (I found mine in an old boxing gym), but they are worth the search because they toughen your skin quickly.

Salt Water Torture

There are herbal ointments on the market that supposedly toughen and heal your skin, but I have never used these products and haven't heard anything as to how effective or ineffective they are. I have always used salt water or just plain salt to help heal my skin after I have gotten carried away and torn off a big patch. I just sprinkle a little salt on the exposed layer of wet meat (is that graphic enough?) and lightly rub it around on the injury. It hurts, sometimes all the way to my elbow, but I have found that it accelerates the healing.

If you are going to toughen your knuckles, I recommend that you only work the skin that covers them. I recently heard of a Japanese master who in his advanced years suffered greatly from all the pounding he did on his knuckles. Arthritis of the bones is natures cruel way of letting you know you did too much when you were younger.

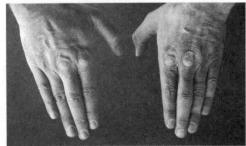

Building thick knuckles is controversial, though some martial artists believe they serve as armor.

to Improve
Your Kicks

I'll admit it, I'm not a great kicker, and any ability I do possess has been hard earned. In bodybuilding, people who develop muscle slowly are called "hard gainers." Well, if this term was used in karate training, I would definitely be labeled a hard gainer as far developing my kicks. Here are some ways I have used to bring my kicking skill to where it is today and has also helped my students become far better kickers than I am.

Hey, who you going to listen to? A guy with natural kicking ability, or someone like me who has had to sweat, bleed and swear for every inch of progress?

1. STRETCHING

There are two basic times to stretch: Before you train, to warm up your muscles in preparation for your workout, and after your training session when your muscles are already warm.

Take it Easy Before Training

Use caution when stretching before your training. Go slowly and gently, keeping in mind that you are only trying to get blood into the tissues and lubrication to the joints. To repeat: This is not the time to work on increasing your flexibility. I've seen many students strain muscles by stretching too hard immediately upon entering the class room. I had a student who tore his hamstring so violently that I heard it snap, and I was in another room. I didn't have any trouble hearing him scream, either. Go easy when your muscles are cold.

Stretching to Increase Flexibility

When stretching to improve flexibility and limberness, you want to first thoroughly warm your muscles with a few easy kicks to a low target, a dozen or so half squats, a dozen reps of leg chambering, and a couple minutes of knee rotations in both directions. You are ready to stretch when you can feel that all the kinks and stiffness have left your legs and hips. Nonetheless, start out slowly and don't push the muscle until you have been stretching for several minutes.

Although, most sports trainers advocate stretching for increased flexibility at the end of class, it's still wise to start out slowly, progressively pushing the intensity of the poses over the 15 to 20 minute session.

You are not "Naturally" Stiff

Don't tell yourself that you are naturally stiff and that you will never be flexible. Even if you have never been flexible a day in your life, you can improve. You just have to stretch consistently, at least every other day. On those days when your muscles feel especially good, push yourself a little, and on those days when you are especially tight, stretch, but take it easy. There will many days when you can't stretch as far as you did the day before. No problem. Just stretch as far as you can and don't worry about it.

Stretching should never be painful. If you have a Marine drill sergeant for an instructor, and he screams, "Push it! Push it! Eat the Pain!" while you are stretching, quit his class. That kind of mentality is dangerous to your health and safety. Stretching is a slow and gradual process that should feel good while you are doing it and leave you energized afterwards.

Be Careful with Partner Stretching

Use caution when stretching with a partner, especially if your partner likes to clown around. I was watching a children's class recently in which the majority of students were goofing around during partner stretching. They were pushing and pulling each other's legs far beyond their maximum capacity and having a good time doing it. The teacher had her head in the clouds and didn't seem to put any significance on the great risk the kids were being subjected to. If I had a child in her class, I would have immediately pulled him out.

While there are the occasional goof offs in adult classes who think its great fun to overstretch their partners, usually over stretching by adults happens by accident. Your partner, who is pushing your leg over your head, can't feel your muscle tension the same way you do. You must communicate to him that your leg is nearing maximum stretch. He may be thinking about the last time the two of you stretched together when you were especially flexible. You must tell him when to slow his push and when to stop and hold it. Don't let your ego keep you from saying "that's far enough."

Keep communicating and keep in mind that partner stretching is never as safe as solo stretching.

Communicate with your partner how you are feeling this day and how far you want to stretch.

Stretching for Strength

Here is a new finding that may surprise you: According to a recent study done by Wayne L. Westcott, Ph.D., director of fitness research at the South Shore YMCA in Quincy, Massachusetts, stretching will actually make you stronger. Westcott conducted a 10-week study, in which 53 people stretched consistently. While all of them made strength gains, those people who followed a complete weight training workout with a separate stretching session showed the greatest strength gains - a 54 percent increase. People who stretched after each weight training exercise, showed a 37 percent strength gain. Those who didn't stretch at all after their weight training, gained 29 percent in strength.

Can you Warm-up for a Street Fight?

Instructor Daniel Alix has found an interesting way to keep his legs prepared to kick hard and fast in a street situation when there is no time or opportunity to warm up.

"Obviously most real fights occur under conditions that don't allow a fighter to warm up ahead of time," Alix says. "I find that a good way for my legs to be ready to perform is to do dynamic-style stretches first thing in the morning.

"What you get from this is a resetting of the nervous control of your muscle tension and length. What this means is that your nervous system has a built-in reflex to avoid letting a stretch, particularly a sudden stretch, end abruptly and cause a tear. It does this by gradually tightening the muscle as it's being stretched.

"Not even intense conscious relaxation will stop your nervous system from regulating the tension in your muscles as they are stretched. What will help is to reset the point where the nervous system starts to tighten the muscle during a particular movement. But don't worry, your nervous system will not allow your tension point to be reset beyond where your muscles can stretch when they're warmed up."

Alix explains the practical application: "To do a dynamic hamstring stretch, raise the leg up to the front. You don't want to throw the limb up in front of you (ballistic stretching), nor do you want to slowly lift the leg up because this forces the thigh muscles to do all of the work. Find a happy medium where the leg still uses its momentum, but at a slow rate of speed. Start out low, then progress higher and higher. You shouldn't feel a big stretch each time; instead you should get to the point where the nervous regulation reflex is about to kick in. You notice that with each lift, the leg goes higher and higher until you reach your maximum height after about 10 lifts. Do a few sets like this to imprint the new nervous reset point (but not too many sets).

"A few hours later, do a few reps of this same leg lift, and you'll find that your nervous reset point is still way up there. You will not achieve this same range of flexibility by performing traditional, stretch-and-hold static stretches in the morning. Dynamic activities require dynamic stretching, while static activities require static stretches."

One last safety tip. When you are at maximum stretch, you should feel a pulling sensation on the muscles being worked. You do not, however, want to feel a pinching, burning or tearing sensation. If you do, stop the stretch or at least back out of it until you no longer feel that sensation. Don't try to tough it out to impress your teacher, your workout partner or because you were able to stretch further during your last workout. Your muscles are communicating to you, so listen to them. Think of this way: If you don't listen to what your muscles are communicating to you, then you must be prepared for some extraordinary pain and many months of recuperation.

Flexibility is Not Just for Kicking High

Greater flexibility not only means that you will be able to kick high, but that will be able to kick faster to a low target. This is because a flexible muscle is one that is looser and less restricted. Also, with a greater range of movement, you are less likely to be injured when you unexpectedly slip on the floor or a sparring partner grabs your kick and jams it up to dump you.

With increased hip and leg flexibility, you can experiment with offbeat kicks such as the reverse roundhouse.

Here Daniel Alix chambers his reverse roundhouse, and then easily snaps it around his opponent's lead leg into his groin . . .

. . . or to his opponent's head

2. SQUATS

Many bodybuilders feel that the squat is the best exercise of all. Powerful legs mean a powerful foundation, a quality we definitely want in the fighting arts.

If you have good knees and you belong to a health club, you can do squats with barbells and various types of squatting machines. As a supplement to your karate training, your objective with squats is to develop fast and explosive leg muscles for kicking, not just big muscles so you can lift even heavier weight. For karate, you don't have to use the extreme poundages that bodybuilders and power lifters use.

If you lift weights and include squatting as part of your regimen, you should squat no more than once a week. Push it hard during your session, but don't squat with weights again for at least seven days. Remember, you are also doing lots of kicking and stance work in your karate training, so don't risk injury by overtraining.

If weights are not accessible to you or you choose not to include them in your training, here are two karate squat-like exercises that work your kicking muscles. Do these at the end of your class or on off days.

Moving Horse

When you are in horse stance, your legs look as if you are riding a big fat horse. The posture is as old as the martial arts and is found in virtually every fighting style in existence.

Some use it as a fighting stance, but I believe that it's too deep and immobile to be of much value in a fight. However, just as there are people who violate "health rules," and smoke and drink into their 90's, there are a few karate fighters who violate "fighting rules," such as tournament champ Bill "Superfoot" who has had an incredible career fighting from the horse stance.

I teach the stance as an exercise position to develop powerful legs, though we never just sit motionless. If you only sit in one position, you only strengthen your legs in that one position. Sitting motionless in horse stance is like doing an isometric exercise where you pit your strength against an immovable object. If that is the only position you do, you neglect strengthening the others. To eliminate this limitation, and to make the exercise more dynamic, squat up and down in the horse stance.

Assume a horse stance with your feet pointed outward slightly, about 10 degrees. They should never point straight ahead as this puts excessive stress on the ligaments and cartilage around the knee joints. As you squat, go as low as you can, but never let your knees extend forward beyond your toes, which also puts excessive stress on your tendons and cartilage. Concentrate on lowering your butt straight down as opposed to bending your knees. You go down either way, but when you *think* about lowering your butt, your knees have a tendency not to extend over your toes as much. Also make sure that your knees always point in the same direction as your toes. If you turn them inward, which is a common error, you put dangerous stress on your tendons. When you have gone as low as you are going to go, push yourself back up and count that as your first rep.

Do one set of 20 reps in a wide stance, but not so wide that you sacrifice your form, and then do a second set of 20 in a narrow stance. That's two sets of 20 s-l-o-w reps.

Sitting in horse is a great exercise but not when held motionless. Instead, sit as low as you can (L) and then slowly come up (R). Do this in sets and reps.

Work only the Bottom Half

If you are feeling especially masochistic, work only the bottom half of the horse squat. Assume the position and lower yourself as low as you can go while keeping your back straight and not letting your knees extend past your toes. This is your starting place. Now, slowly raise yourself half way up and then return back down to your lowest position. Do 20 reps of these, never raising higher than half way. If it hurts too much, take two aspirins, but don't call me in the morning.

After the first few months my students and I did these squats at the end of the class, we noticed a marked improvement in our kicks and - you will love me for this - all of our spouses gave us favorable comments on the nice shape of our legs and derrieres. Cool.

One-legged Squats

If you want a fun workout, don't do these. But if you want one that is a painful killer on your gams and one that will give you fast results, one-legged squats are made to order. If you have bad knees, you should skip this one because it's stressful on the joints.

Hold on to a chair if you need to or, if you have good balance, just hold your arms out to the side. Extend your right leg out in front of you and slowly lower your rear toward your heel. Go down until your squatting leg is parallel with the floor, then slowly push back up.

Start with one set of eight reps for each leg and slowly, over the weeks, work up to three sets of 10 reps. Do them at the end of your class or on off days.

Variation 1:

Assume your fighting stance with your left leg in front and kneel down on your right knee. Maintain your arms in your on-guard position as you drive yourself upward with your left leg and execute a front kick with your right. Snap your kick back and return it to the floor so you are again kneeling on your right knee. Do 10 reps on each leg. If you find these especially difficult, do only five reps on each leg the first week, and add one rep each week until you have a set of 10. You shouldn't do these more than one workout a week, and if you have bad knees, you shouldn't do them at all.

Begin in the kneeling position (L) and then drive yourself up and execute a front kick (R). Drop back to the starting position and repeat.

Variation 2:

Assume your fighting stance but with your left foot up on the seat of a sturdy chair. In one fluid motion, push yourself up until you are standing with both feet on the seat, snap out a right front kick and then set your right foot back down on the floor.

Do 10 reps on each leg. If these are especially hard for you, do only five reps the first week, and then add one rep each week until you have a set of 10. If you have bad knees, skip the exercise entirely.

3. ELASTIC CORD KICKING

I got one of these a few months ago and I really like the constant resistance it provides through the entire range of motion, whether it's a straight-line kick or a circular one. With ankle weights, the poundage and Earth's gravity forces your leg downward. I prefer the resistance to be in the direction of the kick, from the chamber to full extension. The elastic cord gives you that.

When you first strap it on, you might find that it's hard to maintain your balance, but that's a good thing. To keep from toppling over or flying backwards, you must consciously and unconsciously use all your support muscles. This alone will help you develop strong and stable kicking stances.

I do three sets of 12 reps with the front, side, back and roundhouse kicks. Sometimes I do them slowly and other times I do them between medium and fast speed. I'm leery of doing a lot of fast reps because I'm not convinced that it's safe. It may very well be, but when it comes to the joints, I'd rather be conservative. I've broken one knee cap and it's not a barrel of laughs.

The great benefit of kicking with these is that the cord strengthens your movement from the beginning to the end.

4. CLIMBING THE TREE

I made up this name and, yes, it's a stupid one. Nonetheless, it's a good exercise that builds leg and hip strength. Here is how you do it.

Stand in front of your training partner and throw a roundhouse kick at his calf. Retract it into a tight chamber then launch another roundhouse, this time to his thigh. Retract to a tight chamber, then throw another to his groin. Retract to your chamber, and set your foot back on the floor. Those three kicks count as one repetition. Do one set of 10 reps with each leg, which adds up to 30 kicks for each leg, and then allow your partner to have a turn.

On your next turn, add a fourth roundhouse kick to his midsection. Do a set of 10 reps with each leg (now you are up to 40 reps with each leg) and then allow your partner a turn. Add a fifth kick the next time it's your turn, this time to your partner's chest. On the next and final set, add a kick to his head or as high as you can go. All together, you are throwing kicks to his calf, thigh, groin, midsection chest and head, which means you are kicking 60 times per 10-rep set with each leg.

If you began the drill kicking to three targets and progressed as described to six targets on the fourth set, you throw a total of 180 kicks with each leg. If you want a harder workout, use smaller increments as you climb his tree. If you are really full of energy, throw two kicks at each target.

You can make this drill as hard or as easy as you want. The end result is that your kick grows stronger because the exercise requires that your leg and hip muscles do all the work as opposed to momentum carrying the kick to the targets. Try the exercise using all of your kicks.

5. STICKY FOOT

This exercise would be fun if it didn't hurt so much. Its purpose is to strengthen the leg muscles at the point your kick is at full extension, the so-called focus point where the muscles contract.

You can do sticky foot any number of ways: in the air, on a bag, on a tree, on an opponent. It doesn't matter what you kick at because you are not making hard contact. In my school, we do it mostly with a partner, taking turns kicking back and forth at various targets. Here is how it's done using a front kick.

Face your partner and launch a front kick toward his abdomen. When your leg is extended and your foot is touching his body, hold it there for one second, counting "one thousand one" before you retract your leg. You don't need to purposefully contract your muscles, because they are going to do it all on their own - trust me on this.

First, you do the kick and then your partner docs it, continuing back and forth until you have done 10 reps with each leg.

You can kick at any height you choose; obviously the higher the kick the greater stress on the muscles. You can kick slowly, medium speed or fast, it doesn't matter. It's that one-second stick at full extension that you are after.

Do the exercise no more than twice a week using the roundhouse, side, back, hook and crescent kick, and concentrate on using good form.

There is a high potential for muscle cramp with this, so be careful.

A Variation

I was going to call this "A painful variation," but I want to be positive here. This works best if you grab hold of something for support, such as the back of a chair, a wall, or your training partner's shoulder.

Let's use the sidekick to illustrate and let's do it oh so s-l-o-w-l-y. Slowly chamber the kick, slowly extend it, and then stick it at full extension for one second, just as you did with the front kick in the first exercise. Don't cheat and lean too much because you want your legs and hips to do all the work. When the second is up, don't retract your leg; you haven't done the fun part yet. With your leg still fully extended, slowly raise it as high as you can. Yipes! Can you say muscle cramp? If you get one, shake it out and continue with the reps.

Do one set of 10 reps to begin, and progress to another set of 10. As is the case with most exercises, there is no hurry to progress; add a rep whenever you can easily do the last one. Remember, you are trying to *build* muscle, not shred it.

Do this variation with the front, back and sidekick, and you will attack all the muscles involved in most of the other types of kicks. This is a result-producing exercise and, before you know it, you will notice a new crispness to your kicks and greater impact on the bag.

6. 1000-REP DRILL

This will make or break you; the answer lies within you. It's a killer leg workout that will tap your energy, trash your legs and trash just about everything else. But in the end, your kicks will be faster and stronger and your discipline will be ironclad.

Your objective is to do one thousand kicks within about 30 minutes, about one every two seconds. Which kicks you choose is up to you, though you should choose ones that you want to improve. All of the kicks, all one thousand repetitions, must be executed at maximum power and speed. If you cheat and do a few easy kicks, you are cheating yourself and you shouldn't feel pride when completing the giant set.

Here is one version that I have used. Use it or modify it however you want.

1000-Rep Kicking Drill

Single Kicks (Total Reps with both legs: 180)

Technique	Reps	Total Kicks
Front Kick	15	30
Roundhouse Kick	15	30
Hook Kick	15	30
Side Kick	15	30
Crescent Kick	15	30
Back Kick	15	30

Double Kicks Same Leg (Total Reps with both legs: 300)

Technique	Reps	Total Kicks
Front Kick, Front Kick	15	60
Roundhouse, Side Kick	15	60
Side Kick, Back Kick	15	60
Front Hook, Spinning Back	15	60
Crescent Kick, Front Kick	15	60

Supported Roundhouse Kicks (Total Reps: 100)

Hold on to a chair or brace your hand against a wall. If you are doing these with a partner, you can hold hands and kick back and forth. By supporting yourself, you can chamber your kick higher than you can when you are not supported. Do 50 reps on each side.

Unsupported Roundhouse Kicks (Total Reps: 100)

Now throw your roundhouse kicks without support. This way you are using, and improving, your hip strength to get your chamber as high as you can. Do 50 reps with each leg.

Triple Kicks with same leg (Total Reps: 270)

Technique	Reps	Total Kicks
Side Kick, Side Kick, Side Kick	15	90
Front Kick, Roundhouse Kick, Roundhouse Kick	15	90
Side Kick, Back Kick, Back Kick	15	90

Finishing Kicks (Total Reps: 50)

Still got energy left? Whether you said yes or no, you still got 50 more reps to do. Choose any kick that needs extra work and whip out 25 with each leg.

I strongly suggest that you do this drill no more than once every two weeks, especially when you are doing additional training in your school and other exercises in your personal regimen. If you are careful not to overtrain, and it's easy to do with this, you will notice a big difference in your kicks after about four workouts of the 1000-Rep Drill.

Let's conclude this section by taking a look at each of the four basic kicks - round, side, back and front - to see how you can increase your speed, power and overall effectiveness.

7. ROUNDHOUSE KICK - MUAY THAI STYLE

Instead of going over the standard roundhouse kick, let's examine the features of the Muay Thai roundhouse, an extremely devastating version of the kick.

I'm going to do something here that I rarely do, which is to recommend a technique before I have thoroughly tested it. I'm breaking my little rule because in the year I have practiced the Muay Thai method of roundhouse kicking, I've found it to be powerful and fast, more so than the traditional method of roundhouse kicking. No doubt this is why Muay Thai fighters have used this version for eons with great success in the street and in the ring. In fact, they refer to it as "The King of Kicks." Here is how they do it.

Breaking the Rules

One of the primary differences in the Muay Thai roundhouse is that they stand on their tiptoes of their support leg when kicking, especially when kicking to the head. This is considered a sin in the traditional systems and frowned on in many of the modern ones. The argument against it is based on the perceived precariousness of balance and stability, especially when making impact against a bag or an opponent. I tried it and was surprised to discover that it works pretty darn good. More on this in a moment.

Using the Rear Leg

Another difference in Muay Thai's delivery is that they mostly kick with the rear leg, using basically two ways to fire it off. One is to kick with whichever leg happens to be in the rear at the moment a target presents itself, and the other is to do a quick foot shuffle, moving the front leg to the rear and then launching it into the target. This is a deceptive move and a good way to increase the kick's power.

The Mechanics of the Kick

Your kicking foot is launched directly from the floor; you don't lift it into a chambered position before it's launched as many other styles do, but rather send it from the floor directly to the target. As the kick speeds toward its objective, your support leg straightens until it's fully stretched and you are on the ball of your foot. Muay Thai fighters believe that straightening the support leg in this fashion helps the kick move faster and more powerfully, and that standing on the ball of the foot, reduces friction and drag on the floor as it rotates up to 180 degrees.

Your same-side arm is used to help accelerate the kick. When kicking with the left leg, for example, whip your left arm down to your left side and slightly behind you. Your right fist is held on-guard near your right ear.

Okay, here is the four-step process at a glance.

1. Assume a high, right leg forward stance.

2. Launch your rear foot off the floor.

3. As the stationary leg straightens and your foot comes up on the ball and rotates, the hip of your kicking leg begins rotating in the same direction, followed by your thigh, and then the whip-like action of your lower leg toward the target.

4. Contact with the target is made with your lower shin as opposed to the top of your foot.

I like this method of roundhouse kicking, though I will never train to rotate my body 360 degrees as Muay Thai kickers do when they practice in the air. This is because it really hurts when a street thug sticks a blade in your exposed back. But I do like the four-step process, and I find that whipping my arm downward as I kick adds to its power. While it's still hard for me to come up on the ball of my support foot after so many years of being convinced that it's weak form, so far I haven't found anything wrong with it, and it does seem to make my kick a little faster.

Maybe an old dog can learn new tricks.

Free Advice:

Since we are on the subject of legs, let me offer you a little advice that may save you from future health problems.

I'm a strong advocate of kicking an opponent's legs, relating it to chopping down a tree: You hack at the trunk, not at the leaves. The legs are an outstanding target and when specific points are struck, or when any one point is struck several times in a row, the leg will cave in and the attacker will crash to the ground. But, and this a big but, it's not a good idea to pummel your partner's legs in practice.

Yes, I know that Muay Thai fighters do it when they train, and there are stories of some who shin-kick steel pipes and trees in an effort to toughen their legs to

Technique: Roundhouse Kick

Assume an on-guard stance and whip the rear leg into the target.

Note that the support foot is off the ground and the arm has whipped down to add power to the kick, while the other arm is held high to protect the head.

make them even deadlier weapons, as well as to toughen them to absorb their opponent's hard kicks. Does this conditioning work? Yes, it does. Is it good for you? No way. It's potentially crippling in the long run as it damages nerves.

8. SIDEKICK

Here are three ways that Canadian Instructor Michael Holmes gave me to help develop a fast and powerful sidekick. While your particular method of sidekicking may be different from mine or his, you can still incorporate these universal ideas to improve yours even more.

Slow Motion Kicking

"With the sidekick, technical proficiency is vital," Holmes says. "A full-length mirror and a way to support yourself, such as a handrail or a wall, is essential. Strength can be acquired by doing slow motion kicking as you support yourself, and the mirror allows evaluation to ensure proper form. If you cannot kick high, kick low with good form, and with practice and strength development, your kick will get higher. Of course stretching will help, too.

"Practice raising your knee as high as possible prior to pushing your leg outward. This means the kicking foot should travel straight upward before it kicks outward to the target. The higher the knee, the higher the kick will be. Practice reps and sets of this lifting phase slowly, too."

Push with the Toes

I found this little trick to dramatically accelerate the chambering portion of the sidekick. Here is what Holmes says about it.

"Another component to raising the knee, is to push off the floor with the kicking foot when you bring your knee up. To do this, push with the toes of the kicking foot, rather than just lifting or pulling the knee up. The keyword here is *push*. When your leg is chambered in the correct position, knee high but close to the body, you will be able to throw your strongest kick."

Thrust with Momentum

Holmes says to put your entire body behind the kick. "The final component to developing strong sidekicks is the thrust from the chambered position. You are trying to thrust your leg in a horizontal line, parallel to the floor. All your body weight should travel in this same line, which is to say you do not bob up and down. The support leg should drive your entire body mass in the direction of the kick. If you perform a sidekick from a fighting stance with the lead leg, the support foot should move forward at least a few inches from the momentum of the kick.

"To get an idea of the thrusting motion required, begin in a traditional horse stance and spring forward with a lead leg sidekick. Regardless of whether you step forward or hop forward, take care to move in a horizontal plane. If you bob up and down, you will minimize your forward momentum because your energy is wasted moving you up and down. Move straight forward into the target for maximum power."

Michael Holmes thoughts on momentum apply to all techniques that involve a forward thrust. Think of momentum as a straight line of energy to the target. If you allow your head and body to come up and then go back down again when you, say, lunge punch, you break that straight line of energy and you have destroyed your momentum.

Keep your head and body at the same level.

9. FRONT KICK

The muscles you use to execute a front kick get a lot of exercise from your horse stance and any other exercise that involves squatting. Here are three other ways to make this mother of all kicks the pile driver that it should be.

Standing Slow Kicks

You can never go wrong with slow kicks as a way to strengthen the specific muscles that are used for front kicking. Slow kicks hurt and they can be a little boring to do, but they will definitely put power in the thrust. To get the hip muscles involved, the ones that are used in picking your leg up into the chambered position, ensure that you always lift your knee as high as you can when doing slow reps.

Although you should never fully extend your leg when kicking full power, that is, lock out your knee joint, it's recommended that you do so when practicing slow kicking. This ensures that you stimulate the muscles around the knee to keep them strong to protect the joint. Remember the difference: Lock out on the slow kick exercise, but never lock out when doing fast ones.

Do two sets of 10 reps, two to three times a week.

Technique: Side Kick

Assume a fairly narrow horse stance and begin to chamber your sidekick with a hard push of your lead-foot toes.

By simultaneously thrusting your side kick with a thrust of your support leg, you will scoot about three feet. Be sure to keep your head at the same level.

Kneeling Slow Kicks

The motion of your slow kick when kneeling is the same as when standing, but it hurts a lot more. Kneel down so that your right knee is on the floor and your left leg is bent. Hold onto something, grit your teeth and slowly extend your left leg until it's locked out. Retract slowly and replace your foot on the floor. If you get cramps in your thighs, simply shake it out or massage the muscle and then continue with the reps.

Two sets of 10 should be plenty.

Leg Extensions

You need a leg extension machine to do this. If you don't have access to one, you should know that this exercise is so effective that it's well worth the effort to seek one out. It's a good exercise, because the movement with the extension machine is similar to the movement of the front kick, and whenever you can find that feature in a martial arts exercise, go for it.

To save your knee joints, begin the extension not with your legs hanging straight down, but rather with your lower legs extended at a 45-degree angle. Lift the weight and extend your legs out until the knees are locked. Although many bodybuilding magazines recommend that you don't fully extend when doing this exercise, physical therapists disagree. They advise that locking out the leg and holding it there for a one-second count strengthens the muscles around the knee joints.

Don't go overboard with heavy weights. Use a poundage that allows you to do three sets of 15-20 reps. Do this exercise once a week.

10. BACK KICK

The back kick, whether with the lead leg or the rear turning version, involves the largest muscle group in your body - your butt (for some of you this is a really big muscle group, but I'm not going to mention names here). It stands to reason then that to develop a strong back kick you must have a strong tush. While there are lots of exercises that develop your butt muscles, most of them don't put power in your back kick. You want exercises that are specific to the movement.

Before the Actual Kick

There is more to the back kick than just the kick: There is the turn in the turning version and there is the step-up in the straight version, though the straight version can be done without the step. To develop these phases, once again repetition raises its sadistic face. Repeat these preparatory movements over and over until you can do them flawlessly and with speed.

First the straight back kick. Assume a right-leg-forward fighting stance and turn your body sharply to the left. Simultaneously rotate your right foot to the left until your toes are pointing back and your heel is up and pointing in the direction you are going to kick. Lean slightly over your left leg. Repeat for two sets of 10-15 reps with both legs.

To do the turning back kick, turn your upper body sharply to the left as you simultaneously twist your front, right foot on the ball until your toes are pointing straight back. Scoot your left foot on its ball next to your right foot. At this point, your back should be directly facing the target. Do two sets of 10-15 reps with both legs of this partial movement.

Now here are a few excellent ways to develop the thrust phase, the actual kick.

Elastic Cord

Executing back kicks with the resistance given by the elastic cord not only targets the butt muscles, but it also attacks the hamstring muscles on the back of the legs, which are involved in all phases of the kick. At first, your balance is in jeopardy, and you may find yourself being launched in directions you don't want to go. But in time, your balance and coordination will be there and your kick will smooth out.

Don't do the turning phase while wearing the elastic cord or you just might tie yourself up. You are only working on the butt muscles, anyway, so just do the kick.

Do three sets of 10 reps with each leg. Step further away from where the cord is secured as your strength increases.

Slow Kicks

In this exercise, you kick straight back as slowly and as high as you can. When you have reached full extension, hold for a one-second count and feel the intense burn in the ol' cheeks. To add even more intensity to the exercise, push yourself to lift your already locked-out, extended leg just a few inches higher.

To avoid getting physically and mentally stale, do standing, slow kicks for one month and the next month do them from the ground on all fours. Do two sets of 20 - 30 reps.

Horse Stance Squats

Some people think that horse stance squats, which we described earlier, are only for the front of your legs. If you believe this, don't do them for two months, and then do 50 of them in a row. Give me a call tomorrow and tell me what hurts. I know you will agree that horse stance squats work some of the same butt muscles involved in the back kick.

Do one set of 30 reps in a wide stance and do one set of 30 reps in a narrow stance. Be sure to keep your back straight, your pelvis rocked forward and your head held high. Don't allow your knees to extend over your toes.

Bag Work

You can't go wrong including heavy bag work whenever possible. The bag won't lie to you: If you hit it accurately and with good power, it will respond, and if you hit inaccurately, you will lose face. I did that once when I was a visiting instructor in another city. While demonstrating how to kick a swinging heavy bag, I completely missed it and hyperextended my knee. It's hard to be a cool, visiting instructor when you are limping in agony.

Do three sets of 10 reps with both legs and with both methods of back kicking.

Air Kicking

Performing your back kicks in the air is a good way to polish off a workout where you have done several sets of resistance exercises for your back kick. Pick a spot on a far wall and kick at it. Aiming your air kicks at a target will help you develop and maintain accuracy.

If you find yourself falling all over the place when executing the turn, or you are missing the target, slow down and analyze your form. Both problems are often the result of not turning the head quickly enough. First, look at the spot as you stand ready in your fighting stance. Next, execute the spin to a point where your back is facing the target (if you turn too far, you will end up doing a turning sidekick). As you spin, snap your head around to see the target out of the corner of your eye, or at least get a sense of where the target is, and then launch your kick. (see photos at right)

Do as many sets and reps as you like. Occasionally, have a push day where you tell yourself that you are going to do 300-500 back kicks with each leg before you end your training session. You will be amazed at how your back kick will improve - once the soreness goes away.

While in your fighting stance, look at the spot you are going to kick . . .

. . . and spin to where your back is toward the target . At this point, you may be able to see the target, or at least get a sense of it.

Then launch your kick.

to Improve
Your Speed

One time I had a guy attending one of my police reserve defensive tactics class who was blessed with incredible speed - and he had never had a martial arts lesson. I was able to talk him into joining my school, and I enjoyed training him for several months until his job forced him to move. During those few months, his speed never failed to impress me as well as his ability to learn quickly. I would show him a new technique and by the second class he was doing it perfectly and faster than any of my advanced students. On those occasions when he had trouble executing new techniques with good form, it was usually because his natural speed was far ahead of his ability to coordinate the movements, sort of like being too fast for his own good. I had to get him to slow down until he could perfect the overall technique.

Students with natural speed like him are few and far between. The rest of us have to work at it. Here are 10 ways to increase speed.

1. MAINTAIN RELAXED TENSION

I use to believe that to move with great speed, it was necessary for one to maintain total relaxation in the muscles. My theory was based on the fact that when your muscles are tense, thousands of muscle fibers are in full contraction. For example, if you tighten your upper arm and forearm as hard as you can, then launch a backfist, your fist will move like it's pushing through cold molasses. This is because your muscle fibers are already contracted and have nowhere to go.

It seemed logical to me, therefore, that your backfist would snap out much faster if your muscles started out relaxed. Then I met a guy named Bob Munden, a guy with the title, "The Fastest Gun Who Has Ever Lived." Speed drawing/shooting is a modern day sport, in which Bob holds 18 world records. *The Guinness Book of World Records* has timed his draw at less than one-half of one-tenth of a second, less time than it takes you to blink. He draws his weapon completely out of the holster, shoots and re-holsters before your eyes can register his movement. In fact, your eyes see only the re-holster. Sometimes he will shoot the target with a semi-auto handgun, and then shoot the spent shells before they hit the ground. Without exception, he is the fastest human being I have ever seen.

I asked him about my theory of total relaxation. He didn't agree. "My arm and body are never completely relaxed," he said. "If I was relaxed, I would have to come up to the place of necessary tension that I need to be able move fast. When I am waiting for the signal to draw and shoot, my arm and body are slightly tense, in what I call 'relaxed ready.' When I explode, my muscles don't start moving from a place of total relaxation, but they are already primed to move."

Interesting, I thought, and it's hard to argue with a guy who can put a bullet in my forehead faster than I can blink. So, I gave his approach a try using my backfist, which I must say in all humility, is pretty quick. After 10 minutes of whacking the heavy bag and snapping backfists at the mirror, I had to admit that the ol' gunslinger was right. My backfist was quicker when I kept a mild level of tension in my muscles prior to snapping it out.

2. FASTER KICKS

When I see a student's kicks starts to slow, all I have to do is remind him of this simple principle, and he regains his speed almost immediately. Most karate students learn it when they first began studying karate but get lax with it after a few months. If you are one of these people, here is the good news: start applying the principle again and you will immediately increase the speed of your punches and kicks.

Mysterious, aren't I? Okay, here is what I'm talking about. Let's use kicking as an example.

Bring it Back Fast

Simply telling students to kick faster usually doesn't improve their speed. In fact, most strain and tense their muscles in their effort, which slows their kicks even more. This is because the solution is not to kick *out* faster, but to snap the kick *back* faster.

For example, when throwing a roundhouse kick, don't think about how quickly you launch your foot toward the target, but rather think how quickly you snap it back and return it to the floor. To do this, the muscles on the back of your leg, the hamstring muscles, and the cords on the back of your knees, must be in a relaxed state of readiness. Here is a simple drill that will get you moving the right way.

Hot Potato Drill

Face your partner and assume your fighting stance as you prepare to front kick. Your partner hold his palms 12 inches apart in front of his belt, ready to clap. Your task is to launch your front kick between his hands and touch his belt, and his job is to slap his hands against your foot before you retract it. Tell him to be honest and not to clap until your foot begins to retract.

To beat him, concentrate on snapping your foot back as fast as you can. The instant you launch your kick, don't tense your muscles in your effort to return your leg quickly, but rather, *think* about returning it quickly. It may take you a few reps to accomplish this, but once your mind and muscles are in sync, your effort to bring your foot back quickly will in turn make it go out faster. It's pretty darn mystical.

3. KISS

Later, in the section called *5 Ways to Block Faster*, I discuss how your defense against an attack is faster when you have fewer blocks to choose from. This is one of those times where more is not better. There are some mighty fast punchers and kickers out there, so when one of them launches an attack at you, don't stand there and deliberate about the best block for the job.

KISS stands for Keep It Simple, Stupid, with no offense meant. The idea of KISS, as it pertains to the martial arts, is to remind you to always look for the easiest and simplest solution to a fighting problem. Since we are talking about blocks here, I encourage you to throw out the garbage that passes for blocks, and keep the simple but effective ones. If you can block a punch with a simple palm sweep or slap with the back of the hand, why would you choose another way that is more complex? If you can block 10 different hand attacks with one or two blocks, why have 10 different blocks in your arsenal?

A desperate fight in the street can be frighteningly fast and furious. Those fancy smancy blocks won't serve you when you are in a desperate struggle, since your fine motor skills disappear in a quick hurry when fear and adrenaline wash over your body. Keep your defense and your offense simplistic, but strong and fast.

KISS.

Strategy Tip: Keep it Simple

This simple sweep doesn't stop the incoming force but redirects it. From this point, it's a straight shot to his eyes. Keep your blocks and counters simple.

4. DESIGN A SPEED COMBINATION

This is a fun exercise that will make you think about efficiency of movement. I suggest you do this exercise using only hand techniques, but if a kick just begs to be added, go ahead. I don't think you will be as fast, but, hey, prove me wrong.

The exercise involves combining as many techniques as you can into a three-second combination. Use punches, elbows, forearms, slaps, finger gouges, and whatever else you can come up with, and hit with both hands at the same time.

Once you can throw a dozen blows in three seconds, try to do them in two seconds. Once you have achieved that, reduce the time to one second. This necessitates that you be as efficient in your execution as possible. What this means is that you take advantage of every opportunity to hit while you are moving into range and moving out.

Because of your position or angle to the target, there will be some blows that are not going to be powerful. With those, try to strike vulnerable targets. For example, you drive your fist into the target, fold your arm and smash the target with the elbow of the same arm. You can straighten your arm and hit with your hand, but the hit is weak because it's traveling only a short distance with little or no body momentum. Therefore, make your hit a slap to the nose, neck or a finger rake to the eyes, all vulnerable targets not requiring a great deal of power.

You will probably have to modify your combination a few times, adding, subtracting and rearranging techniques as you fine tune it for efficiency (KISS). This is a fun exercise and you will be happily surprised at how quickly you improve

I know of a guy who can deliver 18 blows in a second. Make that your goal.

5. BELIEVE YOU ARE FAST

You are going to like this because you don't get all sweaty and tired. It's all about how you think. Your objective is to believe deeply in your mind that you are already fast, whether you are a white belt or a black belt. You *know* that you are blessed with fast hands and fast feet, and that all your training is making you even faster.

All of the fighters I interviewed and read about when researching information for my book *Speed Training: How to Develop Your Maxim Speed for Martial Arts* said the same thing: You will be fast if you *believe* you are fast. As I worked on the various exercises I wrote about in that book as well as the ones I discuss in this section, my speed improved within a month. But I was also happy to discover that it improved in movements that I hadn't worked on. Amazingly, thinking about being fast and believing that I was getting faster in certain moves was overlapping to other techniques. For the six months it took to write *Speed Training*, I was constantly thinking about my hand techniques being lightening fast, my kicks being quick as a whip and my blocks being imperceptible. While the drills and exercises certainly improved my speed, I'm convinced that half of my improvement came from my thinking about it.

You Perform as you Think

I like the words on a poster I once saw on a wall in a gymnastic center: *Whether you think you can or whether you think you can't, you're right.* I've never thought of myself as being particularly fast. Quick hands, yes, but medium-speed kicks. When I've scored on opponents, it was mostly because I was tricky. I *thought* I was tricky, so I was. I *thought* I had average speed, so that is what I had. But when I began *believing* that I was getting faster and I began acting as if I were fast, my speed increased virtually overnight.

If you meditate, program yourself through self-talk that you are fast now and you are getting faster. If you give yourself affirmations while you are in your car or on the bus, tell yourself what a quick puncher and kicker you are. Tell yourself this at night before you go to sleep, and again when you awaken and your brain is rested, relaxed and receptive to suggestions. Doodle it on your notebook in school, on a note pad when you are on the phone at work, and put sticky note papers on your mirror that read: "I am fast and I'm getting faster. "In other words, convince your subconscious mind by bombarding it with positive statements that you are one fast fighter.

This might sound like some mystical new-age mumbo jumbo, and maybe it is. But it works; you will see a difference.

Oh yes, keep up all your physical training, too. You didn't think you were going to get off that easy did you?

6. REPS IN THE AIR VERSUS REPS ON A BAG

I remember reading years ago about a study conducted in Japan where karate fighters were broken into three groups. One group performed punches and kick against a heavy bag, one group did them only in the air and the third group did half their reps on the heavy bag and half in the air.

After a month, the group that trained only on the bag improved their power but not their speed. The group that trained only in the air improved their speed but not their power. The third group, the one that split their training 50/50, improved their speed and their power. The author of the article went on to say that they experimented further and found that the optimum combination that improved speed and power occurred when reps were done 60 percent in the air and 40 percent on a heavy bag.

Although, I can't recall where in Japan the study was conducted or who did it, I violate a rule of journalism and mention it anyway, because I've found the same results in my training and in teaching others. I know black belts who, for family or work reasons, were unable to attend class or train with anyone for several months. To stay in shape, they trained two or three times a week hitting their basement heavy bags. When they eventually came back to class, they had improved their punching and kicking power but lost speed. On the flip side, I know karate people who have had training periods when they could only punch and kick in the air. They improved their speed but discovered they had lost power when they later worked on the heavy bag.

Train in both areas for optimum improvement.

7. REACTING TO AN EXPOSED TARGET

You can train yourself to react reflexively to your opponent's exposed target just as you react reflexively to his punch or kick.

Have you noticed that when you reflexively snap your hand up to block your opponent's quick backfist, you are able to move faster than when you perform the same block on demand?

You can also see this phenomena when you spar, though it's easier to spot in someone else. Watch someone execute a sweep block against an imaginary opponent when he is practicing in the mirror or responding to the instructor's call. Then watch the same person use the block in sparring when a real opponent is punching and kicking at him at random. The sparring blocks are always faster because the fighter is reflexively responding, as opposed to simply blocking the air.

Offensive Reflexes

When you stand in a line in class and punch the air in response to your teacher's count, your speed will never be as great as it is when you train yourself to reflexively punch at your opponent's exposed target. Yes, fighters punch and kick at exposed targets all the time, but most don't do it reflexively. Instead, they move around until they spot an opening, and then they think something like, "Oh, his chest is open. I think I will punch at it." *Thinking* this slows your response.

But when you train yourself to punch or kick an opening reflexively, you eliminate the conscious thinking process. Your eyes see the opening and your conditioned subconscious directs your technique to explode, sometimes even surprising you.

Here are two drills that develop a reflexive, offensive response to an exposed target. The basic concept is the same with both, so feel free to run with the idea and develop more drills of your own.

Statue

Begin by facing your partner and decide who will be A and who will be B. The instructor says to begin sparring and you both move around stalking each other. When the instructor calls out "Statue!" you both instantly freeze in place, no matter how awkward or silly looking. The instructor then calls out, "A." Since you are A, you strike whatever target B is exposing in his statue position. B does nothing other than be a target. The instructor then orders everyone to move around again. A moment later, he calls "Statue" and then whichever letter he wants to do the attack.

In the beginning, the frozen target holds the position until he is struck. After everyone gets comfortable with the drill, the instructor orders the target to hold the position for only two seconds. Once the two seconds have passed, the target moves and the opening disappears. The objective is for the attacker to hit the opening before it goes away. As everyone gets faster, the target exposer is reduced to one second. Then a half second.

It's a building process that pushes you to react faster and faster as the time gets reduced. The end objective is for your attack to rip into the target the instant you see the opening.

One-sided Sparring

This is similar to Statue except there is no instructor to call out commands. Instead, you and your partner decide who is going to be "It" and you begin moving around stalking each other. Only the person who is It does the attacking, while the other person moves about providing openings. One fighter is It for two minutes and then the other fighter is It for a couple minutes.

As in Statue, the openings at first should be exposed for two or three seconds, and then as both fighters improve, the exposure time is reduced.

Keep in mind that your objective with these drills is to develop offensive techniques that reflexively explode into exposed targets. Keep working them for however long it takes (one week, one month, who knows?) for you to stop thinking, "Oh wow, there is an opening," and to start reacting as if your fists and feet have minds of their own.

8. BLITZ DRILL

Many karate fighters work on developing fast punches and kicks, but they fail to develop speed to close on their opponents. Obviously, a quick backfist won't do you much good if you can't get in close enough to bop your opponent with it.

One dictionary definition of the word blitz is "fast, intensive campaign," which is exactly what you are doing when you charge forward against your opponent with punches and kicks. The Blitz Drill is a fun and extremely taxing exercise that will improve your ability to get from point A to point B. To develop the ability to charge forward like a rocket, you need to train those fast-twitch muscles at least one or two times a week.

You can do The Blitz Drill using any foot work you normally use to move forward. If you have more than one method of closing the gap, use the drill to improve all of them. The beauty of this exercise is that you can do it all by yourself.

Lead-leg Lunge

Lunging forward with the lead foot a few inches followed by the rear foot moving forward a few inches is an old standard used by virtually all fighting systems. Usually, you take only one step to close the distance as you backfist or reverse punch your opponent. But with the Blitz Drill, you lunge five times in rapid succession, crossing several feet of floor space.

Assume your fighting stance, but sink a little lower than you usually do to put more stress on your thigh muscles. As you lunge forward, be cognizant not to raise your body; instead, apply all your energy to the forward thrust. Push off with your thigh muscles, be aware of your overall balance and don't let your head lean too far in any direction. Do five lunges in explosive succession.

Use the Blitz Drill to improve all of your closing methods. Don't punch or kick, but rather use the drill to concentrate only on your blitzing charge. Later you can add techniques, but for now you want to think only about exploding forward five times.

Your goal is to be able to explode toward your opponent so fast that he is overwhelmed by your speed and falls over onto his back.

9. BLITZ AGAINST A TARGET

In this blitz drill, you explode across the gap and drive your punch into your training partner's ribs before he can get away from you. Of course you can only do this if you are fast enough, which is what the drill is all about. Here is how you do it.

You and your training partner assume your fighting stances at the normal distance apart from each other. Your hands are up in your regular on-guard position, but your partner drops his lead arm and holds it behind him. This exposes his front midsection, which is the target you want to punch. Your objective is a simple one: close the gap and punch him in the ribs before he moves out of range, using whatever stepping method you want. Since he doesn't move until he sees you explode toward him, his reflexes get a workout, too.

Hide your intentions by keeping your arms and feet moving as you prepare to explode (I'm using the word 'explode' frequently because I want it imprinted in your mind). To punch at your fastest, move your fist first, followed by a powerful thrust of your front and rear legs to launch the rest of your body (this is why you want to drill first on the exercises in #8). Your partner should tell you if he sees you telegraph.

In just a few workouts, you should be able to beat your partner to the punch. If you want, you can make the drill a little harder by increasing the distance between you by another 12 inches.

Technique: Blitz

Square off with your partner who is exposing his ribs to you.

When he sees you move toward him, he tries to scoot back before you nail him.

10. MISCELLANEOUS REFLEX/SPEED DRILLS

Here are three drills that are as fun to do as they are beneficial to your reflex and speed development. Remember to maintain a relaxed readiness in your muscles so you can better explode when the moment presents itself.

Dropsies

Your partner stands slightly out of range holding a hand pad just above your eye level. You are in your fighting stance with your eyes focused on the pad. When he lets go of it, you react instantly by exploding across the gap and punching the pad before it hits the floor. As you improve, increase the distance from your partner.

Let's Play Catch

This is a fun exercise that will put your nerves on edge. Face a wall about five feet away and let your arms hang down at your sides. Your partner stands a few feet behind you, armed with several tennis balls. His task is to toss the balls, one at a time, over your shoulders and over your head. As the ball bounces off the wall, your job is to reach out and catch it. Immediately drop it, lower your arms back to your sides and wait for the next toss.

This is harder than it sounds because it's difficult to see the balls pass over you. As you improve, your partner can throw them progressively faster. When you really get good at it, you can use different colored balls and catch only selected colors.

You know you have arrived when you can look straight ahead at the wall and catch the balls as they pass over your shoulders. Don't cheat: keep your hands down at your sides until you see the ball in your peripheral vision. One of my arnis instructors could do this easily.

Jerk Away

For this, use the same setup as in Dropsies (photo 1 below), except this time you move first. When your partner sees your forward thrust, he jerks the pad away (photo 2 below). Be careful with this because it's easy to hyperextend your elbow when your punch misses. As you improve, increase the distance between the two of you.

20 ways

to Improve Your Sparring

Allow me to begin this section with my personal view of sparring, one formed after working in law enforcement for 29 years. During those years, I arrested a lot of people, many of whom didn't want their freedom taken away. This always resulted in our thrashing about on the street, across the sidewalk, into trash cans, fences, over the hoods of cars, through closed doors, up stairs, down stairs and in countless filthy and disgusting public restrooms.

How many of those fights do you think happened in wide-open spaces, such as the training area in a typical martial arts school? Not a one. How many do you think went down exactly like a karate sparring match? Nary a one. Never once did the bad guy and I move around, stalk each other and throw sporadic punches and kicks like karate people do when they spar. Instead, the fights erupted in a flash and, in most cases, were over in a matter of seconds.

When I worked the skid row area of town, a place densely populated with winos, thieves, wanderers, mentally ill, murderers, dopers and every other type of violent person (I wrote a book about it called *Skid Row Beat*), I had the opportunity to observe a lot of street people in fights. Most began with the usual exchange of loud words and then, in the blink of an eye, blows rained. Other times, a guy would simply walk up to another guy and a fight began without an exchanged word. Most were over before my partner and I could scramble out of our car.

So am I saying that sparring is unrealistic training? Yes and no. I believe that it has its place in karate training, but I don't believe it should get the emphasis that some schools put on it. I have trained with instructors who incorporated an inordinate amount of sparring in their curriculum because they didn't have sufficient knowledge to teach other things. I have also trained in schools where the instructors included sparring in every training session because they thought they were supposed to, probably because that is the way they learned from their teachers.

We don't do a great deal of sparring in my school because I don't see sparring ability as an end goal. As a street oriented style, why would I want to emphasize sparring after what I just told you about my experience on the street? If I did, I wouldn't be honest to my students; I would be emphasizing something I don't believe in.

I believe sparring is an excellent way to experiment with unstructured offensive and defensive techniques. You learn a new kick or hand technique, you try it in a preset drill with a partner, and then you try it out in a sparring session where you have to use strategy. To me, sparring is only a training device, not an end objective and definitely not a determiner of real fighting ability. This is only my opinion based on my experience.

If you train just for sport, then you should practice a lot of sparring. Just don't confuse competition with street fighting - they are not the same. I've only met one tournament champion who admitted that there was a difference and that he would not trust his techniques on the street.

Here are 20 sparring exercises, drills and training approaches that I have found to work well in my street-fighting approach to karate. Some evolved out of other exercises, and some I learned from other instructors and I include them here because they coincide with what I teach.

If you like to spar just for the enjoyment of it, or you train to compete in sparring, these 20 ways will still work for you, though you might have to make adjustments here and there.

Okay, let's get ready to rumble.

1. DON'T STOP TO DISCUSS WHAT HAPPENED

This is an interesting concept that karate instructor Daniel Alix teaches. It concerns what I call "a psychological catch" that can happen when you focus on what you just did to your opponent or street assailant. Time, even fractions of seconds, are critical in an explosive fight, so don't stop in the middle of it to admire your work, or scratch your head and wonder why your last technique didn't get in. To avoid this, you must develop a mind-set that you must keep on fighting until the street assailant is no longer a threat. For competition, you must train yourself to keep sparring until the judges call for a halt in the action.

One Instructor's Approach

This is what Daniel Alix teaches. "I can remember the first real street fight that I was ever in. I walloped the guy right in the nose and then paused, wide-eyed, with a look of 'did I do that?' on my face. This robbed me of that valuable moment when my opponent was stunned. When you are used to being shocked and worried about striking your opponent in training, you will carry that reflex out onto the street with you. Bad habits in the school become bad habits on the street.

"As you train yourself to continue to fight, your opponent learns how to take a punch without stopping to grab his nose, groin or whatever. Nothing irks me more than to see a student get tapped on the nose and then stop fighting so he can check for blood and discuss it with his opponent."

Alix has a caution for instructors: "Before each sparring session, remind your students not to stop. What happens is that one guy doesn't remember and stops, while his partner keeps kicking and punching. This often causes tempers to flare and strikes to become real.

"One final note: Be sensible about this. If your partner is hurt badly by your attack, you should stop the sparring match."

I had a student who always reacted to being scored on by stopping, shaking his head in wonder as to how he was sucker punched, and then complimenting his opponent. I told him several times not to do this. "Don't give the technique credit," I said. "Keep on sparring when you've been hit." But he just couldn't do it. So I sparred him.

Every time he did his stop, shake and compliment routine, I whacked him with multiple punches and kicks. At the end of our second training session, he was no longer acknowledging my hits, but fighting back.

2. FINISHING OFF YOUR OPPONENT

Here is another good training concept by Daniel Alix that follows up on *#1 Don't Stop to Discuss What Happened.* It's a good concept because it trains your subconscious mind to continue raining blows even after an opponent has been knocked down. Doesn't that make more sense then to stand over the guy and raise your fist in victory as some competition fighters do?

Killer Instinct

"My kickboxing coach used to call it killer instinct," Alix says, "or the ability to finish off my opponent when I smelled blood.' I can't count the boxing/kickboxing matches I've witnessed where one guy could have won if he had possessed a killer instinct.

"I like to work drills that instill in my students a mindset to finish off their opponent. How I usually do this is to have one line be the "glass-jawed" line, that is, the training partner who takes the blow. During a sparring match, the glass-jaw students always go down to the canvas and sometimes even curl up into the fetal position as if trying to protect themselves. The task of the attacker is to develop the instinct to immediately "go for the throat," so to speak. I have found that it's quite common for the attacking students to pause or momentarily blank out, allowing a perfectly good victory to slip away from them. Most had no idea they were freezing like this, and it took this drill to open their eyes."

Alix says you must bring out your savage self. "Keep in mind that you may have to do some mean, nasty and icky things to your opponent. I've dealt with a lot of students who admit that they would have an awful hard time gouging someone's eye or tearing their ear. But they have to realize that they cannot hesitate in a real situation or they might miss an opportunity. Therefore, they must mentally prepare themselves *prior* to being in that situation.

"A particularly difficult student to teach this to is a tournament fighter. When their glass-jaw training partner goes down, instead of jumping in for the kill, they often look to an imaginary judge for a point, or they raise their hands in a disgusting victory pose."

3. USE YOUR SPECIALTY

A good philosophy to have is to be better at your strong points than your opponent is at his. If you are better at kicking than your opponent, then you should use your feet to score in competition or to defeat a street attacker.

In competition, it's usually true that a good kicker is hard to score on with kicks and a good puncher seldom loses by being out punched. This is because each fighter has a deep understanding of his specialty and, therefore, knows all the tricks that can be used against him. By virtue of having practiced thousands of reps of, say his backfist, he knows what an opponent looks like when he is setting up to attack with a backfist.

Some fighters specialize in both hand and foot techniques, but it's rare. When Chuck Norris competed, he was respected as a fighter who could score equally well with his hands and his feet. Usually, though, fighters specialize.

Whatever your specialty, train hard to develop every facet of it.

4. DECEPTION TRAINING

Whether it's one country dumping missiles on another country or two people thrashing about in a filthy alleyway, the ability to deceive is a valuable asset. When you believe that I'm about to punch you in the kisser, but I snap kick you in the groin, I have a distinct advantage over the moment.

Too many fighters train to charge straight into their opponent with their punches and kicks. While this works sometimes, you will have greater success when you use deceptive devices, such as faking, quick-shifting footwork, attacking high and then attacking low, and setting up a pattern of hits and then breaking it, all of which are discussed throughout this book.

To be able to use deception effectively, you must first polish the movements when drilling with a training partner, then work them by yourself and finally incorporate them in your sparring. First work with a partner to ensure that your fakes and other deceptions look believable. A rule of thumb is that a deceptive move is just enough of a real one to fool your opponent. For example, if the fake doesn't extend enough or is launched so fast that it's imperceptible, your partner won't fall for it. (As an aside, I found that drunks usually can't see a fake if it comes at them too fast. When the brain is pickled with alcohol, it can't register fast motion. Slow down your fake when facing a drunk, or don't even bother with one.)

Your training partner should tell you when your deception looks believable and when it doesn't. Once it has met his approval, practice it by yourself in front of a mirror so you develop a good sense of how it feels and how it looks. The last step is to use it while sparring to see how it works in an unstructured format.

5. BROKEN LIMB SPARRING

This is a real eye opener as to what you can and cannot do when you are injured during a fight. The idea is to eliminate one or more of your tools during your sparring exercise. Here are several injuries to experiment with during your next sparring session.

Pretend you have blown an elbow joint in your right arm and you can no longer move it. Hold your arm behind your back or just let it dangle uselessly along your side. In either case, it's no longer available to you offensively or defensively during your match. Now put your left arm out of commission. Again, you can't use it for attacking or defending.

Next, make it a leg that has been injured so badly that you can no longer kick with it, or even support your weight on it to kick with your uninjured leg. In other words, you can't kick at all.

This time it's your right eye that has been injured so severely that you can't see with it. After a few minutes of sparring, open it and close your left one for a few more minutes of eye-opening sparring. Since most people have a strong eye and a weak eye, you will notice a slightly different experience with each one.

Pretending you have an injury is a great way to learn a little more about your capabilities and your repertoire of techniques. It will also mandate that you bend the rules a little as far as body mechanics and the usual way you execute your techniques. It's a time to exercise your creativity.

Real Injury

I encourage my students to keep training even when they have a real injury. For example, I have a tendon and rotator cuff problem in my right shoulder and to a lesser degree, my left. It's a painful problem, but I nonetheless haven't let it stop me from training. When I spar, I either hold my right arm behind my back or I hook my right thumb under my belt. Not only have I not missed a day of training, my kicks and left arm techniques have improved.

Of course, you should never risk injuring yourself more by training through pain. That is not wise and it may lead to an even greater problem. But if you can safely remove the injured part from your sparring, you will gain greater insight into the techniques you have left to you.

6. ENVIRONMENTAL TRAINING

In the section *10 Ways to Train by Yourself,* I discussed the benefits of practicing your reps in places that are cramped, crowded and confused. It's also beneficial for you and your partner to practice your sparring in places other than your usual wide-open training space. You gain a greater understanding of your techniques as to what you can and cannot do in less than desirable environments, which will better prepare you to defend yourself in similar places out in the real world.

In my school, we often litter the floor with students' athletic bags and an assortment of hand pads, kicking shields, hand and foot guards, sticks, and upright bags. I then give the command for everyone to spar around the stuff without moving anything out of the way.

One Other Way

I asked martial arts instructor Marc MacYoung, who has written many books and produced several videos on realistic fighting, how he incorporates environmental training.

"We do what I call melees," he says, "that is, we pit one against one, or two against one. We spar in the back yard, front yard, down the street, over fences, dodging power poles, tripping over dog dishes and patio furniture, dashing between garages, and so on. The only basic rule we have is that we pull our punches and kicks. Basically, we do a running fight all over the neighborhood (it's a good idea, though, to first tell your neighbors what's going on).

"We also do the same thing inside. We spar in hallways, doorways, stairs, bathrooms, closets and basements. It's a great leaning experience."

I remember the first time I fought a guy on a set of stairs. It wasn't pretty because I had never done it before, but being lucky and somewhat adaptive, I managed to come out on top. Another police officer friend of mine wasn't so fortunate - he got thrown over the stairwell railing, hurting his back when he hit the floor several landings down. Practice everywhere and be prepared for the worst.

7. GRAPPLING TECHNIQUES

As ninjitsu was the hot craze during the 1980's, the grappling arts, jujitsu in particular, are the rage now. This is a good thing.

When world champion Benny "The Jet" Urquidez was asked if judo was a good compliment to karate training, he answered, "Knowledge is power. The more you know, the better you can become. Judo teaches you how to fall . . . it makes you very aware of keeping your opponent off balance and how to use his weight against him."

I agree totally. I believe that a student with a black belt in karate and at least a first belt in any grappling style makes for a well-rounded fighter. Of course, a higher belt in a grappling art is even better.

90% of Fights go to the Ground. Oh Really?

Have you ever noticed that most of the people who make this claim are also selling books and videos on grappling? Have you ever wondered where they got that percentage?

This 90 percent claim has not been my experience, nor has it been the experience of all the police officers I asked about it. In all the brawls I had, I can't recall any that went to the ground when I didn't want them to. I'm not saying I was good at preventing it from happening. I'm saying that it simply didn't happen.

I don't want to be misunderstood here. I'm not arguing that fights never go to the ground, nor am I suggesting that you never practice ground techniques. I'm just telling you my experience and the experience of other police officers who have been in many street encounters. I'm also suggesting that you don't blindly accept every claim that experts make, especially those who are selling something.

I strongly urge you to learn ground techniques, because if an encounter does take you to the ground, it's critical that you know how to handle yourself there. It's also important to have knowledge of unbalancing your opponent by tripping, sweeping, reaping, throwing, pulling and pushing.

The Four Ranges

Sparring occurs in four ranges, beginning with kicking range and moving forward to punching range, elbow and knee range and grappling range. A good drill is to flow through these ranges executing techniques in each one. For example, throw a front kick to your opponent's thigh, a punch to his middle, an elbow to the side of his face and finish by grabbing his hair and jerking him down to the ground.

I strongly encourage you to learn at least a few practical grappling techniques. If your style is strictly punch/kick, you need to find a grappling instructor. You can attend a jujitsu school, learn from a friend who is versed in it, or buy books, magazines and videos on the subject.

As The Jet says, "Knowledge is power."

Strategy Tip: Incorporate Grappling

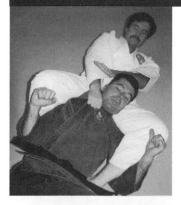

Professor Tim Delgman demonstrates a powerful choke on the ground . . .

. . . and a shoulder- dislocating knee judo lock.

8. MERRY CHRISTMAS

With the possible exception of school yards, the highest percentage of real-life fights occur at night in places of darkness or at least low-light conditions, such as night clubs, parking lots, sidewalks, driveways, alleyways and so on.

Yet you train in a brightly lit school where visibility is always 100 percent. This is another case where training conditions don't match the conditions of real life.

One of the shooting exercises I particularly enjoyed as a police officer occurred at night where the targets were lit only by the strobing lights from atop a nearby police car. While I normally shot in the high 90's in the daytime (higher when we were allowed to score our own targets), my score dropped to the 80's and sometimes 70's when we shot even at close-range targets at night with only the pulsating blue and red lights for illumination. Funny things happened in this weird lighting: targets danced merrily about, gun barrels disappeared in the darkness, and distances became confusing. It was a good course that taught us to concentrate harder and engage all of our senses.

Is there a way for you to practice sparring in lighting conditions similar to what you will find outside at night? Kuntao and silat instructor Bob Orlando uses one that is educational as well as quite festive.

Orlando doesn't emphasize sparring in his school but uses a wide assortment of drills to teach his students the principles, concepts and techniques of his Indonesian fighting style. When he does have them spar, one of the exercises he uses is one that involves fighting in low-light conditions.

"I have two walls of mirrors," he says, "where I string Christmas tree lights. Then I turn off the house lights, leaving on only the small lights around the mirrors. I give the students a few minutes to get use to the new lighting and then they begin sparring."

Orlando's students immediately discover that the same punches and kicks they are so accustomed to defending against when all is brightly lit, no longer look the same in the semi-dark. Distances are hard to judge, the students' timing is off, and they even find themselves backing into other students watching from the sidelines.

"I use a strobe light, too," he says, "and that makes things really interesting when backfists and kicks look like they are coming in slow motion - but aren't. Students learn quickly that they have to rely on their other senses and not just their eyes."

The kuntao and silat instructor usually allows only three pairs of combatants to spar at a time. To add a little spice, he occasionally creates a scenario where three of the fighters are good guys and three are gang members. They start out fighting one on one, but when a "gang member" has the opportunity, he jumps on another good guy, making a two-on-one situation. Sometimes if the opportunity presents itself, there will be a three-on-one fight, and all of this is happening under reduced and distorted lighting conditions.

Give it a try next Christmas or even in July. It's fun and a real educational experience.

9. NO-TAG SPARRING

This is a device that Instructor Daniel Alix uses to ensure that his students are not "tag sparring," that is, sparring the way tournament competitors do. You've seen it: Two fighters square off, move around until one fighter moves in with a quick tag and then retreats.

Should it be Four or Five?

To prevent this, Alix instructs his students to throw no less than five techniques per clash. "This quickly breaks them of tag sparring because they are forced to stay in and keep hitting," he says.

I've had my students do the same thing except they use four techniques. Somewhere, years ago, I came up with the theory that you should not hit more than four times before you disengage. Maybe, I came up with that number because that was the maximum I could throw before I got hit back. Well, no one is going to accuse me of not being flexible: try five hits, then try four. Hey, try six if you want, or how ever many works best for you. Let the situation dictate how many blows you throw before you scoot back out of range.

Working through the Ranges

Besides breaking the tag sparring habit, throwing multiple blows as you move in on your sparring partner gives you the chance to flow with long range techniques, middle range, close range, and then continue hitting as you move back out of range.

This is a good opportunity to use the high/low principle as you move in and out of range. Close the gap with, say, a low kick to the knee, a high hand strike to the head, a punch to the middle, and an elbow to the face - low, high, middle and high again. Hitting at fluctuating levels makes it hard for your opponent to block.

This Works even Better with Pain

If you are actually landing the blows in a real fight, it makes defense extremely difficult for the defender because his mind is so busy moving to where the pain is. When you hit his shin, his brain goes there, and when you follow-up with a face strike, his mind flows to that place. Against most fighters, the third blow to the middle and the fourth to the head usually go unchecked because the brain can't keep up, especially when pain is being inflicted. If you can get a fifth blow in there as Daniel Alix suggests, you will definitely be having a good day.

10. BEGIN WITH ONE FIGHTER DOWN

This method of sparring, also suggested by Instructor Daniel Alix, begins with one person on the ground, either sitting or lying, and the other person standing. I've used this exercise, too, finding it to be a good way to learn how to defend while on the ground and to understand how important it is to get up as soon as possible.

Begin with one fighter down; let's make it you. Lie on your back as if you were just knocked down or you slipped and fell. There is no rule that says you have to wait to be attacked, so roll, slide, scoot, or tumble or whatever way works for you to keep the attacker off. Seize any opportunity that presents itself to go on the offensive. Use your legs to kick, sweep or trip him. Use your hands to grab or punch his legs, strike his groin or to grab something by which to pull yourself up.

If he attacks first, position your legs to protect your groin and use your arms to block and counter strike. When you get an opportunity to get up, do so quickly. It's always amazing to me to see fighters stay on the ground when they don't have to.

Never stand straight up, but rather get up in such a way that you are moving away from the threat. Before the sparring match, experiment with different ways to get to your feet from a seated position and a lying position. Find a couple of methods which allow you to get up with speed, balance and protection against your opponent's quick charge. Practice them repetitiously.

It's imperative that you have an understanding of your offensive and defensive techniques on the ground. I'm not talking about grappling, although you should have some knowledge of that, too. I'm talking about your karate techniques, your ability to punch, kick and block while on the ground. If you have only been practicing them in the standing position, expand your knowledge and your awareness as to what you can do if you suddenly find yourself down.

11. DON'T TELEGRAPH

Teachers often admonish students to not telegraph their movements. "You are signally with your toes every time you get ready to kick." Or, "You always wave your lead hand before you throw your lead jab."

There are so many otherwise good karate fighters who unconsciously tug at the front of their uniform pants before they kick. I remember doing that years ago when I had gi pants that were too tight around the upper thigh. I had to pull them up before each kick because they bound my legs. While this was not a good thing, what was worse was that I continued the habit after I got another pair of pants that were looser and didn't require the tug.

A Bad Habit

It's also possible that some telegraphing habits develop from emulation. A blue belt sees a black belt in his class slap his chest every time he backfists. The blue belt either consciously or unconsciously picks up the trait. One time I asked a new student why he always wiggled his fingers before he reverse punched. "Cause you do," he answered to my embarrassment. "I thought we were supposed to." Woops.

As the word implies, telegraphing means you are sending a message that you are going to do something. If your instructor or training partner informs you that you have developed a habit of telegraphing in some way, you must make every effort to stop. Obviously you can't be sneaky if you are "announcing" your intentions.

Practicing your moves in front of a mirror will reveal telegraphing idiosyn-cracies so that you can take steps to correct them. Another way is to ask your training partner to tell you when he sees you sending out a message that you are about to kick or punch.

Daniel Alix believes that training slowly and building your speed progressively will help you eliminate telegraphing movements. He says: "To teach my class speedy, untelegraphed attacks, I first demonstrate the move at full speed, and then slow speed while explaining the fundamentals. Then I have the students go through the attack at super-slow speed and then gradually pick up the speed. As soon as I see them start to telegraph again, I have them reduce the speed.

"With the backfist, you want to avoid the natural instinct to cock back the arm. To avoid this, you need to imprint the motion into your subconscious. You do this by slowly and repetitiously going through the motion, including leaning the body and lunging with the feet. Once you get your speed up without telegraphing, try it on a bag, against an opponent, in the air, and in the mirror. This is to ensure that the newly imprinted thought is working in more than one situation."

Too much up and down motion can also telegraph a fighter's intention. Alix says, "To eliminate the inevitable bobbing up and down when kicking, I tell my students to imagine they're in a room with a ceiling that is four inches shorter than they are. This helps them break the habit of starting in a nice planted stance, then telegraphing by raising themselves up to kick, then settling back into the stance again."

12. HOW TO THINK BEFORE YOUR TOURNAMENT

Here is a neat little package of things that should be part of your tournament preparation routine. Just as you stretch your leg muscles and shake out your arm kinks, the following steps will link your mind and body in preparation to fight and compete at your best.

Relaxation

In order to begin thinking right, you must be able to determine, in any situation, exactly how you are feeling and what you are thinking. Before competition, or before you are asked to do something challenging in practice, take a good look at yourself. Are you too nervous? Too excited? Not excited enough?

In order to be at your best, at any time, you must be able to achieve a relaxed state. That's not to say you shouldn't be excited or nervous, but you will never achieve peak performance if you are tied up in knots. If you tend to get nervous or overexcited, the first thing you must do before any other preparation is relax.

Here are some simple tips.

• Sit in a comfortable place

• Practice breathing control by counting your breaths for 30 seconds. Then, try to take the same number of breaths in 60 seconds. This will slow your breathing down and help your muscles relax.

• Monitor your pulse: Take your pulse for 10 seconds. Take 10 -15 slow, deep breaths and try to lower your heart rate by two or three beats.

Mental Imagery

This is another great way to help you relax as well as to mentally rehearse techniques, katas or anything you do that needs to be improved upon. I discuss mental imagery in several places in this book, and I encourage you to read them to get a full understanding of the incredible benefits that are possible with it. But for now . . .

• Make sure you are relaxed before you start your mental imagery exercises (go over the breathing instructions above)

• Make sure you see yourself doing your techniques with perfection. See, smell and hear everything going on around you: the sound of the crowd, the smell of the popcorn, the feel of your uniform and the anticipation of the competition.

• Through visualization, recall a perfect fight you had in the past. This will help you remember how great you felt that day. If you can teach your body to recall that amazing feeling before every event, you will learn how to perform consistently at your best.

Cue Words and Positive Self-Talk

Although some people think talking to yourself is a little weird, saying positive things to yourself can be a great way to build or rebuild confidence. Write down some positive cue words and use them during tough practices or at tournaments.

Here are a few most people like.

- Speed!
- Explode!
- Stretch!
- Loose
- Bang!

Self-talk examples:

- "I am strong!"
- "I am totally prepared"
- "I have never been more fit"

Putting them all Together for a Pre-competition Routine

It's important to develop a pre-competition routine using the above suggestions so that you are thinking correctly the day of the tournament. Make it a regular ritual you go through to help you relax and be physically prepared to compete at your best.

- Talk to your instructor about the event

- Do the breathing exercises to relax

- Do the visualization exercise to help you relax and prepare to compete

- Do your usual pre-competition stretching and warm-up

- Use cue words to build your confidence and energize yourself

Be alert to any of these phases that are not working for you and be willing to change them. Practice this routine before every tournament and before any training sessions that you know are going to be especially tough.

13. TRAIN TO GET HIT

I firmly believe that instructors who don't let their students hit each other when sparring are doing a great disservice to them. I've seen schools where students pull their punches and kicks three inches away form their opponents. This is wrong.

Keep this axiom in the forefront of your mind: *How you train is how you will fight in the street.* If you always over-control your punches, not even making light contact, you will do that in a real situation. I've seen it happen.

I'm not talking about full-contact sparring because I don't believe that is the way to go either. You don't have to get hurt or even risk getting hurt to any great extent to learn the martial arts. But you do need to make light to medium impact with your blows to not only know what it feels like to hit someone, but to know what it feels like to take a hit, even a light one.

Learning to get hit should be done progressively. If you are the teacher, few new students are going to stay if you start out whacking them their first day. In my school, I don't allow new students to get hit at all during the first few weeks. Then after a month or so, I start tapping them with punches and kicks while wearing protective gloves and shoes. Slowly, over the next few weeks, I increase the impact to a point where most students can handle medium contact to the body and light to the face.

When I get a student who is especially sensitive or afraid, I build more slowly with him. I might have him stand in place as I move around him tossing techniques at his face and body without making contact. The objective is to reduce his stress and get him to stop flinching. When that is achieved (it might take a few days), I again circle him, but this time I make light contact with the blows. Then a few classes later, I hit him a little harder. Sometimes, I'll have the student stand motionless with his eyes open as I lightly tap his head with my gloves.

Although there are some students who take a month to desensitize, usually it takes only two or three sessions until the average student is no longer afraid of getting struck with light blows.

Work light to medium contact into your sparring. You will be glad you did when you find yourself in a real situation and you don't freeze the first time you catch a punch.

14. DON'T EMPHASIZE SCORING

One of the problems that happens when two people spar is that the session too often turns into a contest to see who can score the most hits. While this is okay, there are also times when scoring should be a secondary objective, the first being to emphasize strategy as to how to make your techniques work against different types of people in different circumstances. You are still sparring to score, but there is a difference.

When sparring sessions emphasize competition-type sparring, the older student or the lower ranked student often gets run over by the younger or higher ranked fighters. In time, the losers get intimidated, frustrated or simply bored, which can result in their dropping out of class. This need not happen; there is another way.

A New Sparring Experience

When you and your partner agree to de-emphasize winning and emphasize using your brain as your ultimate weapon, sparring becomes a new experience. You are more willing to try different things rather than repeatedly using your reverse punch to score. You start thinking how to cross the gap and score with your fast backfist without being scored on, or how you can open up your opponent to your sneaky lead-leg roundhouse kick.

When you train with an emphasis on smart fighting rather than using old standbys to score with, you discover a whole new world of sparring enjoyment. My training partners and I often end up laughing after we try something really absurd. It didn't work, and now we know that. Or maybe it did work and we would have never known if we hadn't had the freedom to give it a try.

Being a smart fighter with an understanding of strategies will stay with you for a long time. If for some reason you miss a couple months of training, your punches, kicks and blocks will get rusty, but not your intelligence. If you suddenly find yourself in a self-defense situation, it will be your brain that saves your bacon. When you do come back to class and begin training again, you will be amazed at how well you spar in spite of your rust.

Post this on your wall: *Your brain is your greatest weapon.*

15. HIGH/LOW

This is one of my favorite concepts, one I have used for years in school, in tournament sparring, and on the street as a cop, empty handed and with a baton. I talked about it earlier, but I want to discuss it again as a sparring device, one that moves your opponent's brain to one place while you hit another. Dirty trick? You betcha.

While there are many techniques that can be applied to this concept, I've chosen two for illustration purposes. Both are effective in street self-defense situations and in competition, though one of them might get you a warning from tournament judges.

Kick Low/Punch High

The first one involves hitting extremely low and then extremely high. Begin in your fighting stance and move about as you normally do when stalking your opponent. When the moment is right, snap a quick kick - front, round, or side - to your opponent's closest ankle without first chambering your leg. Your purpose is not to bash your opponent's ankle, but to hit him just hard enough to draw his attention downward, all the way to his foot. I always try to hit the outside of the ankle when possible, in particular, that round, protruding bone. It's a sensitive target and when struck, gives the opponent a shot of acute pain that not only draws his attention there but keeps it there.

Making contact to a low target in competition may get you in trouble with the judges, so you should make the kick a quick fake to the ankle. If it's quick with no contact, you might get away with it.

A split second after you have hit or faked to his ankle, throw a punch to your opponent's face with a snapping lead-hand. It's a fairly easy punch to get in because your lead hand is so close and his attention is drawn downward.

I often follow the high head punch with another low blow, such as a snap kick to the groin. His busy brain is going low, high, and then low again. If things are going well, I'll throw one more high blow to the head. As I mentioned earlier, I've found that most people can't keep up with four high/low blows because their brains simply shut down. Trying to keep up with the extreme levels is just too overwhelming.

Punch Middle/ Backfist High

Here is another technique applied to the high/low concept that has earned a lot of points in tournaments for a lot of fighters. It's also a good technique on the street when executed with speed, power and good target selection.

Assume your fighting stance and face your opponent. Never stand statically, but stay in motion so your opponent can't see when your attack begins. Move from right to left, forward and backwards and keep your arms moving. When the moment is right, launch a punch at your opponent's ribs. If he doesn't fall for the bait and block it, he gets hit in the ribs and then you follow with a backfist to his face. If he does block the middle punch, immediately launch your backfist to his chops. It doesn't matter what he does because he always gets hit.

Instructor Michael Holmes uses the high/low principle when he teaches the importance of throwing multiple blows when sparring. He has found that emphasizing multiple hitting is helpful for those students intimidated by sparring, because it forces them to stay in range and throw blows rather than hitting once and scampering away. Here is what Holmes says about it.

"When attacking, always use multiple strikes and keep on striking while in-range. Too often, people throw one or two techniques, and then halt to see if their attack worked. This can be suicidal if the opponent has blocked the initial blows and the attacker is still in range.

"A further complication happens when beginners or intermediate students bunch their techniques to the same target, such as throwing only head shots. Instead, it's better to punch high, then follow with a medium or low attack. No one can cover his entire body; there is always something open."

Holmes recommends that you attack with a flurry of blows to various targets. "The idea is to keep your opponent busy blocking so he isn't hitting you. Sooner or later your blows will penetrate his defense. One way to practice is to shadowbox, that is, fight an imaginary opponent, emphasizing striking to various levels and angles.

"Another way to train is to have your partner not hit back but only defend as you try to overwhelm him with repetitive blows. When you can do this easily, have your partner defend as well as counterattack. Your final stage is to incorporate this method in your freestyle fighting.

"The concept is simple: If you bunch your techniques together, it's easy for your partner to block them. But the value of this concept becomes self-evident when you stagger your blows to high and low targets."

High/low works. Use your favorite techniques to create your own combinations.

16. I CAN HIT YOU BUT YOU CAN'T HIT ME

In this drill, you and I spar but you can't block my blows and you can't punch or kick me back. Obviously, this is more fun for me than it is for you.

While I move about and stalk you (be afraid, be very afraid), you bob and weave, twist and turn and shuffle forwards and backwards to avoid my hitting you. You can accomplish this by getting in close and jamming me, by angling, by staying away or by scooting out of range.

This is a great exercise for your footwork as you move about trying not to get hit. Your mistakes might hurt a little, but your learning will accelerate when you move the wrong way and catch one of my killer blows. A nice benefit is that you will quickly understand how staying in motion provides you with some degree of control over the match. Of course, I'm not going to make that easy for you.

17. SPAR WITH A VARIETY OF PEOPLE

All too often when the instructor tells the class to spar, the same people always pair up. There is comfort in doing that, but there isn't a lot of growth going on. It's better to spar with a variety of people to experience the many different ways fighters move, punch, kick, block, and plot their strategy.

Once because of my job, I was limited to training with only one person for a month. I didn't realize how I had gotten use to his particular way of throwing his backfists, roundhouse kicks and reverse punches until later when I sparred with another person. I had a hard time with my new partner because his angles of attack were slightly different, his way of moving threw me off guard, his timing felt odd, and his speed and power were different.

Look for sparring partners with these differences.

• Spar with a fast fighter to learn what to do against speed.

• Spar with a powerful fighter to see what happens when his techniques crash through your blocks.

• Spar with a slow fighter to see what happens to your timing.

• Spar with a partner who doesn't acknowledge your hits but keeps fighting.

• Spar with a partner who fights street, not tournament, style.

• Spar with a partner who throws a lot of combinations so you can examine your defense.

• Spar with a partner who fights linearly, and spar with one who circles.

• Spar with a sloppy fighter who disrupts your timing and the execution of your techniques.

• Spar with a white belt whose techniques are not as clean as a higher-ranked fighter's.

• Spar with people of different body sizes: weight, height, and reach.

World Champion kickboxer Kathy Long prepares for a 12-round fight by sparring four partners, each for three rounds. Because each new partner is fresh as she progressively gets tired, and each one fights a little differently, she is forced to pay close attention to her footwork, strategy, and her offensive and defensive techniques.

18. DIAGONAL STEPPING

This works great against fighters who always spar in a straight line. It's also effective on the street against an attacker who charges straight at you, flailing his arms in a desperate attempt to land a punch on your nose.

Imagine a large X on the floor. As you face your opponent, imagine that you are standing in the middle of the X where the lines cross. Your opponent is in front of you between the top of the lines. From your position in the middle, you can step forward diagonally left or diagonally right, or you can step backwards, diagonally left or diagonally right.

Stepping for Defense

Diagonal stepping works great for defense. For example, when your opponent lunges toward you with a reverse punch, you can respond by stepping diagonally forward either to the left or right as you block. This places you out of the line of your opponent's trajectory and in close range to easily counterattack him. If he thrusts a front kick at you, you can move away from him, either diagonally back to the left or to the right and counter with whatever technique works best.

Stepping Offensively

Offensively, I like to suddenly step diagonally forward, say, to the left with my left leg, leaving my right leg trailing. My opponent's attention is drawn to the sudden shifting of the large mass of my upper body, so I take advantage of that momentary visual distraction and whip my trailing leg across his thighs.

The four directions remain constant, but how you use them is up to you. I keep my stepping patterns simplistic because I'm a simple guy who likes to do things the easy way. Feel free, however, to experiment with more complex stepping patterns, and be sure to do them with speed and have fast offensive techniques to add to them.

For diagonal stepping, tape the floor and face your opponent between the lines.

When he lunges forward with a punch, step diagonally as you block.

If he launches a kick, step diagonally back and block. Stepping diagonally removes you from the trajectory of the attack.

19. FIVE ELEMENTS THAT WILL MAKE YOU A BETTER PUNCHER

There are dozens of excellent strategies you can use to make your punches more effective, but no matter what methods you use, your technique requires at least five of the elements listed below. You notice that I don't make these absolutes and say you *must* use this stance, or you *must* move this way. There is never one way to do karate, because we all have different physical structures, different ways of moving and different ways of thinking that make up our individuality. What I offer here are basic principles that enable you to get in and score. You have to experiment to see which of your favorite techniques best apply to them.

Your Feet should be Fast and Mobile

Some fighters like to move around on the balls of their feet like a boxer, while others prefer to move about flat footed. Experiment with both positions to see what works best for you. You may find, as many others have, that a combination is effective. What is important is that you have tested both and can move fast in the one you choose.

Keep your Upper Body Moving

Along with your trick footwork, keep your upper body moving forwards and backwards, left and right, and keep your arms in motion using short, jerky movements.

Keep your Guard Up

I've discussed before in this book the importance of keeping your guard up. If you are going to throw a backfist and your lead hand is down, it's going to take time to raise your arm to launch the attack, and the motion will telegraph your intentions.

Keep your guard up so you can launch your backfist on a straight line, which is always the fastest path to your opponent.

Thrust your Feet Forward

There are different ways to thrust forward. One fighter thrusts off his back foot a split second after he launches his hand attack, while another drives forward with his lead foot first, followed by a thrust of his rear leg. There are also occasions when a fighter lunges forward with his lead foot and leaves his rear foot planted. This is okay as long as he knows that it leaves him rather stretched out and vulnerable.

Experiment with all of these variations to see what works best for you. What is important is that your fist leads the attack followed by a powerful thrust with one or both of your legs.

Total Commitment

Have you seen fighters start to throw a technique then stop because they didn't have the confidence to carry through? Their lack of commitment caused them to lose an opportunity to score.

Your opponent is not going to stand there with his arms and legs spread wide and say, "Hit me, dude." You have to either make an opening happen, or find one that happens by chance. By whatever means a target is exposed, you have only milliseconds to seize the opportunity and blast it. Remember, a lost opportunity is, well, a lost opportunity.

For many fighters, a lack of commitment comes from fear of getting hit. Yes, you *might* get hit, but one thing for sure is that the more you worry about it, the greater the chance you *will* get clobbered. Try this experiment. The next time you run up a set of stairs, think about the mechanics of putting one foot in front of the other and how careful you need to be to not fall. Woops! You fell didn't you? Sorry about that, but I had to show you that sometimes too much thinking and too much caution can be detrimental. This is especially true when launching an offensive technique.

There is your opponent's head and there is a clear path to it. Throw that backfist NOW.

20. CLINCHING

Let's say you end up virtually chest to chest with a guy who is pummeling away on you as if he were getting paid by the punch. Or he has pushed you against a wall and is pressing against you as he does his best Elvis Presley, lip-curling snarl. Whatever the circumstances, sometimes clinching is the best option to prevent a guy from hitting you and to tie up his arms so you can hit him with elbows, knees and close punches. Here are three ways to clinch.

Both Hands Behind his Neck

This is one of my favorite methods because you can control your opponent, keep your upper body protected from his punches and pull him into your knee strikes. You need to weaken him quickly with your blows, because the hold on his neck isn't that hard to escape from, especially if he is strong.

Get both of your hands behind his neck (don't interlock your fingers) and press your forearms together in front of your body. Place your head close to his and watch for his punches so that you can adjust your forearms to catch his blows instead of using your tender tummy. Pull down on his head to tire and control him, and jerk him around like a dog does with a rabbit in his mouth. Muay Thai kickboxers like to throw their opponent's to the side with this clinch, sometimes so effectively that their opponents fall to the ground. Before you throw him, though, drive your knees into his upper thighs and midsection. If he tries to block you with his arms, smash your knees into forearms and upper arms. Any target struck with a bony knee hurts.

One Hand Behind the Opponent's Neck

You can start out with one hand hooked around the back of his neck, or use it in the event he pulls your other hand off. It's a strong technique because you have one hand on his neck to control him, while your other hand is free to block his punches, trap his hands and punch him with short blows.

Jerk his head downward and try to keep your left forearm in front of your upper body for protection against his punch to your chest or abdomen. Use your right hand to stick to whichever arm of his is the most dangerous. Don't hold onto it, because you want your hand free to punch an opening or block a blow. Just stick to it and go wherever it goes. When an opening appears, punch it with your free hand. And don't forget to use your knees when the opportunity presents itself.

Clinch his Arms

This one is harder to maintain than the other two because you are only sticking to your opponent's arms, rather than holding onto something.

Use this against a guy who is holding both of his arms in front of him. Place both of your hands over his wrists. Don't grab his wrists with your hands, but instead hook yours over his. Press your weight against his arms and stick to them as much as you can. When you have an opportunity to punch or claw, go for it. Remember, you have minimum control with this clinching method and it's fairly easy for him to escape from it. Use this only for a short duration as you seek an opportunity to create distance from him or move into one of the other clinches.

Technique: Clinching

Hook your wrists over your opponent's wrists and press your weight against them to control her arms.

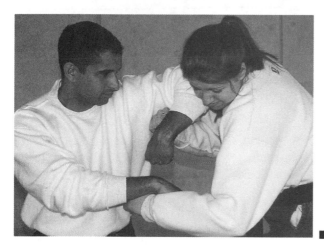

When the opportunity presents itself, whip an elbow into the side of your opponent's face.

to Score Almost Every Time

Some people might call these methods tricks, gags, or gimmicks. By whatever name, they are clever and sneaky ways to get your fist and foot into your opponent's opening. They are tricky because they don't rely on brute strength or blinding speed to get in, but rather manipulation of your opponent's thinking process.

When you control his mind, you control the openings.

1. DRAWING

"I think of this as bringing the mountain to Mohammed," says Instructor Daniel Alix. "When sparring, you retreat, retreat, retreat, and then you stop and lunge forward into your opponent who has been following you. This works great for scoring with a hand attack, because it's easier for the person retreating to spring forward than it is for the aggressor to stop and move back. Besides, the aggressor's mind won't be on defense, it will be on offense because he is busy chasing his opponent."

I've always called this concept *drawing* because as you move backwards, you are pulling or drawing your opponent to you. He may be throwing a couple techniques as he advances, or he may just be stalking you looking for an opportunity to attack. In either case, he is thinking offense because he thinks he has you on the run.

Technique: Drawing

As you move about stalking your opponent, move backwards and subtly gesture with your finger tips for him to "come here."

As strange as it seems, more times than not it works. When he steps forward, lunge forward and drill him

Yoo hoo! Come Here

If you get an opponent who doesn't follow you, try making a little "come here" gesture with the finger tips of your lead hand. It's a subtle movement, a wiggling of your fingers for him to come to you while at the same time, you move backwards. The gesture of the fingers and your backward body motion has a psychological effect on your opponent (many opponents, but not all) making him feel compelled to follow.

Once you get him moving forward and you have taken three or four steps backward, stop abruptly and explode forward with a pile-driving punch. Time it so that he is taking a step forward as you make your sudden change in direction. If you do this in a tournament, he walks into the point, your point. If you are in a street situation, his forward motion adds even more impact to your blow.

It's mandatory when doing this that you *explode* like a rocket into the guy. I've had opponent's actually jump because they were so startled by my sudden change in direction. But watch your control with this in class and in competition. I've seen some training partners hurt by poorly controlled blows.

2. CREATE AN ILLUSION OF DISTANCE

There are lots of ways to create the illusion of being farther away than you really are. The idea is to make your opponent feel comfortable, make him lower his guard consciously or unconsciously, and then hit him.

Here is a way to sneak in a backfist that I learned from Professor Rick Alemany, a kenpo stylist in San Francisco. It's based on the concept of broken rhythm but with a twist at the end. First, Alemany tries to set up his opponent to believe that he is too far away to connect. Just as his opponent begins to think he needs glasses, Alemany explodes into the surprised man's face with a backfist that seems to come out of nowhere. Here is how you can do it.

Square off with your opponent in your fighting stance just outside of hitting range. Move around as you usually do when sparring and throw out a backfist that falls far short of hitting. He will either reach out to block it, or just ignore it if he has good depth perception. You throw out another backfist, again too far away. By feeding your opponent deliberate misses with the same technique, you established a rhythm, a pattern in his mind that says you are too far away to make contact with him.

131

Strategy Tip: Deceptive Distance

As you spar, condition your opponent's mind by throwing two backfists that miss by several inches. Do not step forward when throwing them.

On your third backfist, cross your rear foot over to your left behind your stationary lead foot, and surprise your opponent with contact.

Third time is "gotcha" time. Say your left leg was forward when you threw out your first two backfists. On the third one, step to the left with your right, rear foot behind your lead leg, almost as if you were falling backwards. Although, your left foot doesn't move at all, just as it didn't move with the first two backfists, your rear leg sidestep puts you within range. Snap out your left backfist and laugh to yourself as you score a perfect hit against his surprised face.

Camouflage the move even more by keeping your body in motion, especially your arms. It's harder to detect the backfist when it's launched out of motion rather than from a static stance.

3. FIGHTING RABBITS

Don't you just hate sparring guys who scoot out of range every time you kick at them? You have fast kicks, too, but against the above average fighter who can hustle backwards like a quick rabbit, you just can't get them in.

Tests How He Reacts

Try this the next time you have one of these guys. First launch a backfist at him, move around a little, and then throw a reverse punch. Most likely, the guy didn't rabbit away from your hand techniques but stayed rooted and blocked them. Just to make sure, throw another hand technique. Yup, he just blocked and countered without moving back.

You have just gathered some intelligence data: He runs from kicks, but he stays set and blocks hand techniques.

Now Get Him

Here is how you can set up this guy so you can connect with your kicks almost every time. Begin by moving around as you normally do when sparring, and launch a fake backfist to imprint the idea of 'hand technique' in his mind. He will either flinch from it or overreach to block it. Move around some more and launch another fake backfist. Again the guy stays in place and starts to block, but this time you quickly retract your fist as you simultaneously chamber your front leg and drive home your fastest kick.

If you had started with that kick, the guy would have run away. But because you know he doesn't run from hand techniques, you set him up with a backfist to keep him in place so you can score with your kick.

4. THE THREE STOOGES TECHNIQUE

A self-defense philosophy that I have always held is this: If an assailant can't see, he can't attack you. While it's not a terribly profound philosophy, it's definitely true.

If you have ever been poked in the eye, you know what I'm talking about. Your eye slams shut, tears flow, your nose runs and your other eye shuts partially or all the way in a sympathetic response. The pain is acute and your entire being at that moment is focused on your eye. Indeed, the only thing you want to do is moan and clutch your face.

A guy tried to tackle me one time when I was working as a police officer. His tackle didn't take me down, but he was able to wrap his arms around my legs in an embrace so tight that I was on the verge of crashing to the sidewalk. I'm not that skillful on the ground and as a police officer wearing a gun, I didn't want to go down and be at risk of losing my weapon. I had to act quickly.

I flicked his closest eye with my fingertips. He instantly released his death grip on my legs and dropped to the sidewalk, clutching his face and yelping like a kicked dog. It worked like a charm.

There are a variety of ways to strike an assailant's eyes.

You can . . .

• gouge with your thumb

• poke with your index finger

• thrust with your index and middle fingers

• claw with all five fingers

• rake: left to right, right to left, upward or downward

You don't have to be Arnold Schwarzenneger to poke an assailant in the eye because strength and power are not important, nor are stances and proper body mechanics. I know this is true because all three of my kids poked me in the eye when they were babies lying in my arms (when the third one did it I began thinking conspiracy). Sometimes speed is critical to the deliver of your technique, but other times it's not an issue. The only element that is necessary is accuracy.

Out of a Clinch

Try this experiment. Lock arms with your training partner in a standard clinch and then jostle around with him. When you feel a weakness in his grip or you see a clear opening, shoot your fingers toward his eyes. It was an easy score because you didn't need to rotate your hips, set yourself in a specific stance, or wind up your strike. You simply went from where your hand became free and shot it straight to your partner's eyes.

Off a Block

I like to use eye strikes off of a block. My opponent throws, say, a reverse punch and I slap it away. At that moment of contact, my blocking hand is my closest weapon to my opponent. Without cocking my arm, retracting my hand or doing any other kind of preparatory movement, I simply claw, gouge or rake his eyes. And I can do it faster than he can blink.

On the Ground

Say you are on the ground and the attacker is getting the best of you. He's got you locked up so effectively that you can't use your punches and kicks. If you can manage to loosen one of your arms, or if the attacker's head moves in close enough, seize the opportunity and touch his eyes with extreme prejudice.

The Three Stooges were masters of the eye poke. With practice and an eye for seeing an opportunity, you will be just as good as they were.

And there isn't anyone who can tolerate the pain of an eye poke.

5. INVISIBLE KICKS

I got the idea for so-called invisible kicks from an article I read in the Feb./Mar. 1998 issue of *Karate International*. In the article "The Quest for the Perfect Kick" author Dr. Larry Sanders mentions a martial artist by the name of Nei Wai Chia who uses "ghost kicking." In a nutshell, this is any kick or combination of kicks the opponent can't see because his view is somehow obscured by his body or the kicker's body.

I have used these kicks for years - I've always called them "invisible kicks" - but until recently, I never organized them in any fashion until the article gave me the incentive to do so. Once my senior students and I began devising invisible kicks, we found all kinds of ways to do them. The only thing we couldn't figure out was why we hadn't organized them earlier.

You Can Do Them from Any Position

Invisible kicks can be executed directly in front of your opponent, behind him, or off to the side just far enough to where you are out of sight. To make your kick invisible from the front, you must first obscure your opponent's vision, which is usually done by blocking his eyes with your arm or his arm. For example, block his punch and then push or pull his arm so that it covers his vision, and then kick any target from his ankle to his jaw.

To get behind him, you need to block his attack as you simultaneously move to his rear. Once there, and out of his line of sight, simply kick whatever target is available. If you can't get all the way around behind him, move to his side and forcefully twist his upper body just enough so that he can't see you. At that moment, and it may be only a brief moment, kick whatever target "begs" to be kicked.

While the name invisible kicks may sound exotic, there really isn't anything fancy about them. All you need is a little creativity and you will find lots of opportunities to use them. And it's fun to watch your opponent look around and ask, "Hey, who kicked me?"

Block your opponent's punch and step diagonally to the outside of his arm.

By pushing his arm across his face, you have momentarily blocked his vision. Seize the moment and hook kick his kidney.

Still out of sight, pop him with another kick by bringing your heel up sharply into his groin

6. THE INITIAL MOVE

No matter how lightning quick your backfist or how explosive your kick, you won't hit the target unless your initial move is fast and deceptive. With practice, you can close the gap between you and your opponent or assailant so quickly that he has no chance to elude, block, jam, or counter your attack.

There are two ways to close the gap. We have discussed deception in several places in this book and how to use techniques like fakes and the high/low principle. This time, let's look at how speed can be used to get from point A to point B. We have talked about some of these elements in other sections, but let's look at them again to see how you can use them to launch yourself like a rocket on your initial move.

Use a Mobile Foot Stance

When your feet are set wide, your ability to move is reduced. It may be stable and look dramatic, but to move, you must take the time to bring your feet together. So, why not start with them closer?

Place your feet under your hips similar to the position boxers use. This eliminates your having to adjust your feet or shift your bodyweight, which alerts your opponent that you are up to something. You still face him at roughly a 45-degree angle, but as you move around, your feet maintain a distance about the same width as your shoulders.

Stay Moving

If you are not convinced that your stance should be mobile, try this easy test. Have your training partner stand in his stance without moving his feet or his arms, and then have him lunge forward and throw a combination at you. The next time, have your partner move around - bobbing, weaving, shuffling his feet, moving his arms - and then attack with that same lunge and combination. Quite a difference, isn't it? An attack launched from movement is much harder to detect than an attack launched from a static stance.

Throw a Few Fakes

Although we are talking about raw speed, your attack is going to be perceived as even faster when you manipulate your opponent's mind by using deceptive movements, such as short feints, partially chambered kicks, short thrusts of the shoulders and even bobbing your eyebrows.

If your initial attack is really going to be a lead-arm jab, first throw a couple of partial ones. You want to see how your opponent reacts to your attack, and you want to condition his mind to believe that your real jab is just another fake.

A simple faking technique I learned from Professor Rick Alamany is to mix real and fake backfists to the head with real and fake reverse punches to the body. Whichever one your opponent falls for, you simply hit him with the other. It works like a charm.

Your Hands Move First

When your initial move is, say, a backfist, your fist needs to move first (by the way, as an initial move, hand attacks are usually faster than kicks). A common error I see students make is to lunge their bodies forward until they are close enough to attack with their backfist. Worse yet, are those students who execute their hand attack at the same speed their body moves forward.

Both of these methods are poor ways to attack. Moving your body first alerts the opponent that you are on your way. All he has to do is wait until you are close enough and then bop you in the nose. Backfisting at the same speed as your body moves forward, is the slowest of all ways to move. Think of it this way: On a good day you can move your body about 25 MPH, but on that same good day, you can move your fist about 90 MPH. So, why would you backfist at the same speed your body moves?

A Revealing Study

One study showed that a fighter who moves his body before his hand technique, can only move about 12 inches before he is detected. But a fighter who launches his hand attack a split second before he moves his body can cover as much as four feet with his attack before his opponent reacts.

Keep Your Hands Up

I have always been puzzled as to why some fighters move around with their arms down at the sides. Not only does it look peculiar, it's next to impossible to get off an effective initial move. When your hands are down and you want to punch, you have to bring them up, which is a waste of time and a warning to your opponent that a punch is on the way. Also, it's impossible to fake or use other deceptive hand moves when your arms are hanging lifelessly at your sides.

Keep your hands up, keep them on guard and keep them moving.

Strategy Tip: Hands Move First

Imagine an invisible string tied to your wrist and the other end tied to your ankle. Launch your backfist by moving your hand first.

About ½ to 3/4 of the way to the target, the string tightens and pulls your foot forward into a lunge step. Your fist should land and retract before your foot lands.

Maintain a Poker Face

Besides maintaining a blank face when you attack, you need to be careful of little subtleties, such as gritting your teeth, inhaling audibly, squinting or widening your eyes, tugging your pant leg and wiggling your fingers. Practice your attack in front of a mirror to ensure you are not giving away your intention.

Don't Hesitate

I talked about this earlier when we looked at the issue of commitment to the attack. Just remember that the slightest pause can cause you to lose an opportunity or get hit. You need confidence in your ability to score, confidence derived from the hours you have invested in practice. Don't think about getting hit on the way in, think only of scoring with that explosive initial move.

7. ALWAYS HIT WHEN IN RANGE

Have you ever been to a tournament and seen two fighters square off with their lead hands virtually touching? Or have you ever seen two guys in a bar stand chest to chest and taunt one another? Hopefully, you were never one of these people.

I can still hear my first instructor telling us over and over to stay away from our opponent unless we were hitting him. "If you're in range, it's the first person to hit who gets the score," he told us repeatedly. "Stay away from the guy unless you are hitting him."

I've always hammered on the same point with my students, whether the situation is competition or self-defense, but I add this: If you are close enough to hit, then do so - but don't stop hitting until you or your opponent has moved out of range. If you can easily throw six punches in a second (though you should be able to throw a lot more than that), and you are in range for one second, you should be hitting your opponent at least six times. But if you only hit him, say, three times in the first half of the second and then stop, you are vulnerable to getting hit by him in the last half of the second.

When you are in range, fill the time with your blows. If you don't, he just might fill the time with his.

Keep this thought in mind: It's better to be the hitter than the hittee.

8. FOOT SWEEPS

I learned foot sweeps many years ago from Dan Anderson, a top-rated tournament fighter throughout the 1960s, 1970s and 1980s. I was his first teacher in 1966, and he stayed with me through brown belt. I had to go into the army when he was just getting into competition, and when I got out he was a black belt and making his mark in a big way on the tournament scene. He went on to be one of the top 10 fighters in the country.

I ended up learning from him, including how to sweep. The first time he did it to me, however, he swept *both* of my size elevens so hard that my body went up into the air horizontal with the floor. The going up part wasn't so bad, but that unceremonious crash on the floor really hurt.

For our purposes here, the word *sweep* means you knock your opponent's foot far enough away from his stance that it momentarily throws him off balance. I'm not talking about dumping him on the floor, although if it happens, that's okay. Most of the time, though, you will upset his balance just enough so that you can quickly take advantage of his momentary distraction.

Most people have a natural fear of falling (except for those darn jujitsu guys). When you sweep your opponent's foot, you spark a startle reflex within him. For just a moment, and it's usually a very brief moment, he is concerned about falling. He is not thinking about you, but about himself, and it's during that distraction, which lasts no longer than a fraction of a second, when you want to punch or kick him.

In my school, we have a rule that you can only sweep the outside (little toe side) of the opponent's foot. This is for safety reasons because when a sweep is delivered to the inside it's easy to connect kneecap to kneecap, which is right up there in the Top 5 list of things that really hurt. On the street, however, anything goes.

Sweeping is made easier when you set up your opponent by removing some or all of his weight from his closest foot. One easy way to accomplish this is to thrust your lead palm against his shoulder to knock him back a little, thus relieving some weight from his front foot. Another way is to force him back with a charging face punch. Whatever way you do it, the instant his foot lifts, go for the sweep.

Since the defense against a sweep is for your opponent to simply lift his leg, you must practice executing the technique with great speed. It's best to break it down into stages: the setup using evasiveness, the foot sweep and lastly the follow-up hit.

But no matter how fast you get with it, it's hard to use it more than two times on a smart fighter. My senior black belt, Gary Sussman is quite good at sweeping since at 6'4, his legs can reach you from across the room. "I've always found it hard to sweep an experienced fighter more than once," Sussman says. "Because it startles him so much that first time, he is usually ready for any future attempts. You might sneak in a second one if you set him up right, but a third is next to impossible if he is at all skillful."

Once perfected, foot sweeps work almost every time because of the built in natural fear human beings have of falling. Seek his startle reflex, and then punch or kick him hard. Don't dillydally with your follow-up because his startle reflex only lasts for a brief moment.

9. PUSHING AND JAMMING

All fighters use some kind of fighting stance from which they launch their offensive and defensive techniques. At the very least, a fighter's stance might have him standing straight up with his feet together and his arms at his sides as if waiting for a bus. Although this may not be an ideal fighting stance, it's quite possible to block and attack from it. At the other end of the spectrum is the sophisticated karate stance where the arms are positioned in an on-guard position and the feet are staggered in some fashion.

No matter what fighting stance a fighter uses, the hard part is penetrating it with your attack without being blocked. With the concept I call Pushing and Jamming, it doesn't matter how your opponent positions his arms because you are going to just push one or both of them out of the way, anyway.

The position of your opponent's arms serves two functions: to guard his body and to be a launching pad from which he throws his attacks. When you push or jam his arm or arms aside, you momentarily take away his ability to strike with his hands and you clear a path so that you can strike with yours.

How to Set it Up

You can use all kinds of fakes to set this up, although I make it work almost every time by using a simple and direct-line lunge straight into my opponent's guard. Here is how it works.

You and your partner assume your fighting stances with your left sides forward. Your plan is to jam his lead hand and follow with a punch to his face.

143

Strategy Tip: Set-up the Sweep

Push his lead shoulder to remove a little of his weight from his lead foot and then quickly sweep it away.

He will only be concerned about falling for a second so punch him quickly.

Your punch is launched simultaneously with your push or, at the most, it follows a fraction of a second after. Keep in mind that you need to get your hit in instantaneously because your opponent is going to recover quickly and cover his opening.

When the moment is right, lunge forward with your lead foot, thrust your lead palm against his lead hand, and push it into his body. Simultaneously (or almost), fire your right reverse punch into the opening created by your push. Snap your punch back and continue with additional blows, or scoot yourself out of range.

You have to be Quick

Try to explode into the guy so hard and fast that it startles him, which clogs his thinking and slows his reaction. Don't raise your head and body as you lunge forward. This telegraphs your intention and slows your forward thrust. And don't lift your jamming hand or look at the hand or arm you are going to hit. Strive for efficiency and eliminate all unnecessary movement.

Jam vs. Push

A jam occurs when you forcefully press his arm against his body. I like this because it gives your opponent a mild and brief sense of helplessness as you punch the tar out of him.

You push your opponent's arm when you move it any direction other than into his body. For example, you can push it to the right, left, up or down. Since your fist is only four or five inches wide, you need to push it only a few inches to clear a path for your punch.

Usually, the push or jam is done with your lead hand although there are times when your rear hand is the best option. For example, if your opponent likes to extend his lead arm, push it down with your rear hand and smack him with your lead backfist.

You can also push his lead and hit him with a kick. Say he favors extending his lead arm toward you in his fighting stance. Push it aside and whip in a fast roundhouse kick to his groin.

Practice by yourself in front of a mirror to ensure that your lunge and hand movements are as efficient as you can make them. Speed is all important with this, so push yourself to go faster and faster. When you progress to working with a partner, it's important that he allows you to do the complete technique so that you can polish all elements of it. Once you feel you have it down,

145

incorporate it into your sparring.

Pushing and jamming an opponent's guard is an excellent way to penetrate a defensive guard when he isn't being nice and giving you an opening. It not only disrupts him physically, but it jams his thinking for a brief moment as well.

It works almost every time, but only if you are quick.

10. THE HALF STEP AND SUCKER PUNCH

This is a tad bit similar to *#1, Drawing* but different enough to warrant a separate category. I think of it as a way of suckering your opponent into feeling comfortable enough to counter after you have hit or attempted to hit him. This concept doesn't work against a fighter who turns and runs when you attack, or against a masochist who stands still and lets you hit him. It works best against a fighter who blocks or evades and then moves in for a quick counter.

The Set Up

You and your opponent assume fighting stances with your left sides forward. You initiate an attack by lunging forward with a backfist. If it hits him, fine. You scored. But if he blocks it or in some way evades, you immediately take a half step back. Since he is an adamant counterpuncher, he lunges forward, right smack into your second backfist.

Taking a half step back is a little unusual since most fighters attack and then stop, leaving themselves vulnerable to their opponent's immediate counter. By your taking a half step back, you create distance and give yourself a moment of safety from his automatic counter. He can still hit, but he has to first take a step to reach you, which is what you want him to do so you can catch him with a second backfist.

This also works with a kick. Drive a front kick into his middle, he blocks or evades, and you step back a half step so he can't get you with his immediate counter. When he lunges toward you, drill him with another front kick.

Your second technique doesn't have to be the same as your first, though I made them so in my two examples. It can be anything that is quick and applicable.

Technique: The Set Up

You snap a too-far-away backfist, which the counterpuncher easily evades.

You half step back quickly before he can counter you in range. But since countering is in his blood, he lunges forward to cover the short gap.

Feel free to laugh as he walks right into your backfist. Great speed is essential to make this work.

to Improve your Blocking

Let's face it, training to develop good blocking skills is not as exciting as leaping into the air and launching two double kicks (leaping like this would be exciting to me because I would break my neck). But here is the bottom line: If you aren't successful in blocking your opponent's attacks, all your cool moves won't mean a thing when you are lying on the floor counting the tiles in the ceiling.

While the physical act of blocking is one that should be simple, the subject is actually somewhat complex. You need to understand when to block and how and when to involve your body in the block. There were many times in my early days in karate when I thought I had my blocking down, only to come up against fighters who could snap a backfist and whip out a roundhouse kick as quick as a wink and humble my feeble attempt at not getting hit.

I began training in a Korean style that had blocks similar to many traditional Japanese styles. They were smashing-type blocks designed to inflict injury on the attacking limb (though they always hurt my arm, too). I was too dumb in those early days to notice that even though we spent countless hours slamming out thousands of those robot-like power blocks - inside, outside, upward and downward - not one student used them when we practiced free sparring. Hello? We never questioned this but just blindly followed the instructor's teachings. After all, the blocks worked like a charm when we used them in our *prearranged* drills.

If you are convinced that one or more of the blocks your instructor is teaching is not doing the job, talk to him about it. It could be the way you are executing them, or it might be that the block is worthless.

I've seen some ridiculous blocks that look good in the school, especially when you know what the attack is going to be. But I would bet your left kidney that they would never work in the harsh reality of a back alley street fight. I know, I've been in a few back alleys (Saigon, Vietnam was one tough back alley) and learned the hard way.

If you don't get satisfactory answers from your instructor, seek out good blocking techniques on your own. If your instructor protests, change schools. Hey, it's your skin you need to protect, not his ego.

While I'm not going to get into particular blocks here, I'm going to suggest five ways to improve the ones that you are using. Keep working on your double jump kick if you want, but also work hard on your blocks so you have the opportunity to use it.

1. LIMIT THE CHOICES

When I began training in karate back when dinosaurs ruled the earth, I learned a different block for each type of kick. The sidekick got this kind of block, the roundhouse got that kind of block, and so on. Ridiculous as it seems to me now, we were expected to choose the right one when a surprise kick sped our way. No wonder I was always getting whacked with kicks in those early years.

In my school today, we have reduced the choice to just one lonesome block that can be used against all kicks aimed at the groin and above. Here is how it works. Let's say a roundhouse is thrown at your left side. To block it, drop your slightly-bent left arm to the outside of your body and support your forearm with the palm of your right hand. If the kick comes at your right side, drop your right forearm to your right side and support it with your left palm. The support hand isn't always necessary for straight kicks, since they are mostly being deflected, but we always use it against circular types, like roundhouse, crescent and hook kicks, where your block is more of a force-against-force type.

If the kick is aimed at a high target, we again block with the forearm but with the blocking hand up and with our palm supporting the arm as we lean slightly away from the incoming force. I think of the defense as a fender protecting a BMW's expensive body - mine. Since the support palm in both the low and the high block is positioned close to the attacker, it can be used for a quick backfist counter.

Technique: The All Purpose Block

You block the roundhouse kick with a supported block . . .

. . . and then step forward to deliver a quick backfist to the head with your support hand.

This one block works against most, if not all, kicks to the upper half of the body. You just have to adjust your footwork a little depending on the type of kick and its trajectory.

If you don't like this particular block, that's fine (I'll just have to deal with the rejection), just change it to whatever way you prefer; it's the concept - the reduction of choice - that is important. The fewer choices you have, the faster and more effective you will be.

Let me repeat that: *The fewer choices you have, the faster and more effective you will be.*

Now that I got you thinking about making fewer choices, take a look at the blocks you use against hand attacks. Choose a couple of your favorites and see how many different attacks you can block with just one or two.

2. STUDY THE ORIGIN OF THE ATTACK

This is a fun drill that is a real learning experience. By *origin of the attack*, I am referring to the initial stage of a punch, strike, kick or major body movement, that moment in time when your opponent changes from stalking you, to launching his attack.

Let's say his intent is to throw a backfist. He is shuffling around when suddenly his lead shoulder tilts toward you followed by his big hairy backfist rushing toward your face. For the purpose of this exercise, you don't care about that rushing backfist, but rather the tilt of his shoulder, that slight movement from where the attack originated.

I don't believe in all those old stories of ancient masters who would intuitively know what attack was coming their way. It may have seemed to the uneducated eye that they had some kind of mystical sixth sense, but I believe their real skill was in detecting the origin of the attack, and then knowing what would follow. They had educated their eyes to perceive and translate their opponent's slightest movement.

You can do this, too, but you have to work at it. Here are a couple ways to get started.

Make use of your "Dummy" Time

You probably practice drills in class where you and your partner square off to work on an attack of some kind. The way many schools practice is to have one partner throw a technique or a combination while the other partner stands there doing nothing, other than acting as a dummy to the attack. After 10 reps or so, the roles are reversed.

This is a waste of time. Instead of the dummy partner twiddling his thumbs, he should use the moment to study the origin of his partner's attacks.

Let's say you and your partner are working on a front kick drill. When it's his turn to kick, use the time to study his body movements to see what occurs microseconds before he thrusts his foot. Can you detect movement in his shoulders, his waist, his hips and his support leg? Memorize these subtle, or not so subtle actions, and then later compare them against those that occur in your opponent's sidekick, roundhouse kick and so on. Learn what movements are indicators of each specific kick.

153

Partial Rep Drill

This is a simple drill that allows you to focus only on one small phase of an attack. Let's say you decide to work on the reverse punch, and your partner is going to punch first as you watch. From his on-guard position, he executes just the first two inches of the move, which is nothing more than a very slight forward roll of his shoulder, a slight forward movement of his fist and a slight backwards movement of the opposite hand. He repeats this as you watch, letting the image imprint into your brain. After he has completed 10 reps, it's your turn to throw 10 partial punches. It's a good idea to throw a couple of completed punches at the end so that your brain links the partials with the reverse punch. Be sure to do the exercise on both sides.

Use these origin-of-attack exercises for as many offensive attacks as you want. It won't be long before you know what is coming a split second before your opponent launches it.

3. SIMULTANEOUS BLOCK/COUNTER

This has always been one of my favorite blocking concepts, primarily because it saves time and it can be psychologically disconcerting to the attacker. Here is how it works.

When your opponent throws a backfist at your head, the usual way to deal with it is to block and then counterattack. Block *and then* counter. With simultaneous block/counter, there is no *and then*. Instead, you snap your arm up to block the backfist *as* you drive a punch into the attacker's ribs.

All hand attacks can be simultaneously blocked and countered as can all kicks above the groin. Kicks to the thighs, knees, shins and ankles are harder to block/counter but not impossible. Low kicks are usually blocked with your shin, which makes reaching the attacker with your hands difficult since he is usually too far away. It's possible, however, to do a simultaneous *evade*/counter by waiting until the opponent's low kick is a couple inches away from, say, your shin, and then jerk your leg up and out of its path and turn it into a roundhouse counter.

Your simultaneous block/counter can be quite startling to your attacker. When he decides to throw a reverse punch at your face, he launches it with full expectation that it's going to reshape your nose. But just when he expects his fist to hit you, your fist hits him. This can be so disconcerting to some fighters that they stop attacking.

Just as your opponent expects his punch to make contact, you make contact with your block and kick.

One time a second-degree black belt in taekwondo joined my class. This guy had beautiful kicks and could easily pop them over the head of my tallest student. During his second night in class, he told me, in somewhat of an arrogant tone, that he wanted to spar my senior student. I agreed, but I said I wanted him to first spar Annie, one of my female green belts. His mouth spread into a smile of superiority as he looked down his nose at her. He began to anxiously pull on his gloves.

"Every time he pops one of his high kicks," I whispered to Annie, "block it and simultaneously slap a kick up into his groin."

She smiled an evil smile, and said, "No problem-o."

The sparring session lasted about three minutes before the black belt got frustrated and called it quits. Every time he snapped one of those beautiful kicks to her head, she blocked it and simultaneously kicked his groin or knee, landing them with nice smacking sounds. After a minute of this, he lowered his kicks, but still she block/countered them. A minute later, he stopped kicking and tried to score with punches, but she was right on the mark with, you guessed it, block/counters again. After the third minute he quit and never came back to class.

He may have learned a lesson, but I lost a dues-paying student.

4. BLOCKS ONLY DRILL

This is a simple little exercise that improves your ability to block in just a few workout sessions. Square off with your partner and decide who is going to attack and who is going to defend. Let's begin with you defending.

Your partner begins attacking you at slow to medium speed, throwing everything at you that can defend against at your level of training. If you are a black belt, he should throw everything including a frisbee; if you are a white belt with just a couple months of training, your partner should limit what he throws to just a couple hand techniques and two or three kicks.

In either case, your job is to block without countering. He is stalking, circling, moving in and out of range, all the while throwing kicks and punches. He never lets up, but maintains a steady barrage of blows at the agreed upon speed. Your task is to block, evade, bob and weave. You will miss some, but don't stop to say "Ouch!" Just keep on blocking nonstop for 60 seconds. When the time is up, it's your turn to attack while he defends.

Make sure you stop the blows. I'm not talking about smashing the guy with your blocks, but knowing that your sweeps and checks are doing the job. All too often, students give token slaps at an attack and only *think* they are blocking successfully. Make an agreement with your partner that if either of you sees that the other is not blocking properly, the attacker will try extra hard to penetrate and make contact.

Consistently getting hit with the same attack is a good way to know that you are blocking improperly. I was doing this exercise with a student recently who kept nailing me with reverse punches to my stomach. I thought I was blocking them correctly, but it's hard to argue the point when her fist kept hitting me over and over. Thanks to this drill, I figured out what I was doing wrong.

Don't let consistent misses continue without analyzing the problem - and correcting it.

5. WHERE TO LOOK

If you ask 10 karate instructors how and where you should look at your opponent to best see his attacks, you will get at least three different answers. "Watch the hands," "Watch his eyes" or "watch his solar plexus." This has been a longtime controversial subject that doesn't need to be controversial.

When I use the words see and look, I'm really talking about perceiving the action, not necessarily looking right at it. You don't have to actually see a kick to block it. If you have at least a sense that a kick has been launched at you, that is sufficient for you to respond.

I have discovered that there is no one place to look that works for everyone. For example, I recently read about a high-ranking karate fighter who teaches students to look at their opponent's midsection to best see everything his hands and feet are doing. So I asked a couple of my black belts to try it. A few minutes and a few bruises later, they both reported that looking at each other's solar plexus didn't work for them; they kept getting whacked over and over. (I'm glad I had *them* try it first.)

The first three years I trained, I found it effective to look off to the side of my opponent, using my peripheral vision to detect his attack. But the higher I got in rank, the more trouble I had making it work since my training partners were also getting higher in rank. I especially had trouble using it against exceptionally fast fighters of equal rank to me.

A lot of fighters recommend focusing on the opponent's hands. Sometimes this works, sometimes it doesn't, depending upon how deceptive the opponent is. For example, watching his hands can get you into trouble if he is good at faking, blocking your vision, and using his hands to distract you from his quick kicks.

Look at his Triangle

For the past several years, I have suggested to my karate and police students that they focus their gaze at their opponent's chin and shoulder area. If you draw a line from your opponent's right shoulder to his left and then a line from both shoulders up to his chin, the lines form a triangle. When you look in the area of the triangle, you can see and perceive *everything* he is doing. You don't have to look down at his feet because you know they are directly underneath his shoulders (unless he has a really weird body). When he begins to throw a lead roundhouse kick, his lead shoulder lifts slightly and his rear shoulder dips. When he begins to throw a reverse punch, his rear shoulder rotates forward. You can even perceive his toes wiggling when looking at his triangle.

The triangle concept may not be to your liking, though it has worked for everyone I have taught it to. If you have given it a good test and it still doesn't work for you, then you need to try something else. Perhaps the solar plexus is a better focus point for you, or maybe watching the elbows, like at least one kung fu style suggests.

Since you can't defend against what you can't see, you need to find a way to look at your opponent so as to perceive all of his attacks. I suggest you begin with the triangle.

10 ways
to Improve
your Kata

In the last few years, the subject of practicing kata has become more and more controversial as teachers and students question its value. Is it helpful or is it a waste of time? Since I have the soapbox here, allow me to comment.

During my first three decades of training, I loved kata, doing it almost daily, competing on a regular basis and winning lots of gaudy pieces of plastic. I defended its importance for years. I pushed my students to practice theirs, and I required that they demonstrate them for every belt exam. I even wrote a book on how to train and compete with kata called *Winning With American Kata.*

But I began thinking differently about it a couple of years ago. I was having trouble justifying the time and energy needed to perfect kata movements, many of which are abstract, flamboyant or just plain silly. If they were so effective, why didn't we use them in sparring, class drills and in self-defense? And my katas are simplistic compared to the acrobatics seen today in kata competition. Would you really ever use aerial cartwheels, backflips or somersaults in your school sparring, tournament fighting or, heaven forbid, in the street?

In short, I have changed my thinking to believe that all the attributes you get from kata training - focus, concentration, accuracy of delivery, speed, power, mobility, ability to change directions, and others - can be developed from the hundreds of fighting drills that exist in karate training. And you get them in a far more realistic format.

In my school, we always strive to make our training efficient and realistic. To achieve this objective, I use drills and exercises that are *directly applicable* to fighting rather than using a choreographed "dance" of techniques.

If you remain in the fighting arts as long as I have, you will discover that you pass through many phases of how you view your training efforts. What I just expressed about kata is where I am today in my approach to karate. Your situation may be different. If you practice kata because it's required in your school curriculum, you like to compete in tournaments or you just like doing them because, well, you just like them doing them - don't let me change your mind.

Will practicing kata help you fight better? Yes. Are there other more effective and efficient exercises and drills that accomplish the same thing? Yes there are.

But if you are still reading this section, my guess is that you are interested in making your kata better. Here are 10 ways that will do just that.

1. SOFT PRACTICE

As the name implies, soft practice is a method of performing your kata slowly, at about the same speed as a tai chi form. It's a time to integrate your mind into the movements, to *feel* each one and to totally focus on every minute detail.

Proceeding slowly and softly allows you to evaluate your kata to ensure that each movement is absolutely precise. It's a time to strive for deeper stances, sharper techniques and to feel the rhythm that is in the kata. Take the time to see the battle that is unfolding before you: the charging enemy, their kicks and punches and the effects your blows are having on them.

Though you are moving no faster than a falling leaf, use the same mental intensity in each of your techniques that you do when executing them as hard and fast as you can. Feel your blocks make contact with the attackers' arms and legs. Feel your punches and kicks make contact with their bodies. Feel, feel, feel. See, see, see.

2. HARD PRACTICE

This way is not for wimps. It's a real calorie burner, but it will greatly improve your speed and power.

Physically, you are to proceed through your kata from the first move to the last, pushing for greater speed, more power, extra explosiveness, deeper stances and a laser-like mental intensity. The underscored word here is push.

Mentally, you work yourself into a controlled rage that grows more and more intense each time you go through your form. Your neck cords bulge, your eyes burn, your muscles burst with energy, and your mental intensity burns white hot. By the fifth time through, you are an enraged animal and pity on anyone who gets in your way.

Am I overstating this? Not at all. You might even scare yourself a little. But in the end, you will own faster and stronger techniques and have a greater ability to focus mentally. You will probably lose some quality of technique because you are pushing so hard, but that's okay. To recapture any lost form, simply finish your workout by doing your kata a couple times at regular speed.

In the end, you will feel a great sense of pride from knowing you have pushed yourself to your limit, physically and mentally. You will have surpassed what you thought was your top speed and power. You will have smashed through a barrier and will have grown from the experience.

That's a real nice feeling.

3. SECTIONAL TRAINING

I think this is one of the best ways to get a kata in shape quickly, whether it's for a belt examine or a tournament. The concept is simple: Instead of going through your kata in its entirety, break it into several sections, performing each one several times before you move onto the next one. This worked wonderfully for me during my competitive years and I'm convinced my 50 trophies, some of which are grand championships (aw shucks, it was nothing, really), are a result of training this way. Here is how you can do it.

Breaking it Down

If your kata has 100 movements, break it into four sections of 25 movements each, or really break it up and reduce it to 25 sections of four movements each. Most likely, though, the sections will contain an uneven number of techniques. For example, there might be three sections of three movements, two sections of eight movements, four sections of two movements, and so on. This is because you want to follow the natural flow of the kata, especially when there are built in pauses.

Since most forms have a counter for every attack, make it a rule to never break after blocking your adversary, but rather break after countering him. You can also break right after the last move before a change in direction, or on a dramatic built-in pause.

Sectioning allows you to give total concentration to a handful of techniques that need work. If one section is problem-free, do it only five times. But if the next section is causing you problems, work that one 10 or 15 times. It's a lot easier to do a small section 15 times or even 25 times than it is to do the entire kata 25 times, especially if it has 100 or more moves.

Sectioning is the most result-producing training method I found during my years of competition. Give it a try and send me a picture of you and your trophy.

4. UNDERSTAND WHAT YOU ARE DOING

As a kata judge, there is nothing that annoys me more than watching a competitor go through his form as if he were thinking about what he wanted for lunch. You are in a fight for your life, madly defending against attacks from a half dozen to ten assailants coming at you from every direction. This is not the time to be thinking about lunch.

I've seen this attitude in tournament competitors as well as in students in class who perform their kata techniques without an understanding of what each movement means. Even worse, is when a student understands, but fails to execute his techniques with any sense of a fight. If you don't know what a movement means - for heaven's sake find out.

To get value out of practicing kata, and to increase your chance of winning in competition, it's imperative you understand the purpose of each punch, strike, kick, block and step. When you understand the target you are hitting and the attack you are blocking, you will do so as if your life depended on it.

Even if you don't like kata, train yourself to think of it as more than "something you have to do" to get promoted. If you have to spend the time and energy learning a form, make sure you have a complete understanding of what you are doing - fighting. FIGHTING. Convince your mind that you are in a real fight and, in no time at all, your kata will have a whole new life and a whole new value to you.

5. MENTAL INTENT

During my first years of kata competition, I was able to learn a great deal about presentation, especially mental intent, from watching champion Karen Sheperd perform and reading her thoughts in various magazine articles she wrote.

Before I proceed, let me say again that kata training is not just for competition or belt promotion but also for your own enjoyment. Many of the performance elements that are important in competition, such as mental intensity, are also important in helping you enjoy doing your kata outside of the tournament ring.

Here is what Sheperd says about bringing intensity to your kata, whether you are doing it in your backyard or in front of a tournament audience. "In kata you're also working with your emotions," she says. "That's probably one of my strong points - my ability to project through my eyes. I'm talking about the anger and excitement you feel when you intend to win. You should radiate this strong, positive energy as though you were trying to hypnotize the judges with your confidence that you are going to win."

Sheperd believes in the importance of a positive mind. She says, "One of the main tasks is to overcome the negative energy out there in the ring. People walk out into the ring and you can practically see it all around them. It's like they are saying, 'Everybody's watching me. I'll just go through the moves and get it over with.' You can feel the negativity around them. To win, you've got to push through all that and grab for that positive energy that maybe somebody gave you before you left home. Maybe you have friends there with you from your school who really believe in you.

"You have to grab on to the positive energy and learn to perform within it."

6. THE DRAMATIC PAUSE

Many kata performers fail to separate the scenes in their forms, as if they have no idea where a confrontation with one opponent ends and the next one begins. They rush through their kata like they were doing one, long, multiple-technique.

To add a greater sense of drama to your kata, pause briefly when you have finished with one attacker. Let's say that you finish off the guy who came at you from the front and your next move is a turn to your left to meet another attacker. This is a great place to put in a two-second pause. To make it even more dramatic, make a quick look to the left before you turn or at least appear to be sensing the approaching attacker. Too often, a kata performer simply turns and blocks the attack coming from his left as if he has eyes on the side of his head. I grade a competitor down for this because it's obvious to me that he is only turning because his kata calls for it, not because he has any sense of a threat coming from that direction.

Their Importance

Think of the pauses in your kata as being just as important as they are in music. Music without them would just be noise, and a kata without them is just one long combination. Where to pause depends upon the kata. In traditional forms, pauses are usually established, so any individual interpretation is discouraged. Modern American freestyle forms, however, are more open to personal inter-pretation. In my forms, there are usually one or two places where pauses are mandatory, but I leave it up to the student where he wants to add any others. Hey, it's his fight.

Since my forms are all 100 moves long, there is a greater opportunity for cre-ativity than there is in forms with only 25 movements. Sometimes I interpret the form by blending Scenes One and Two before I pause briefly. Then I do Scene Three and pause, and then I blend Scenes Four, Five and Six and then pause for a longer beat. I continue this way through the entire kata. The only rule I have is that I only pause after I have executed an offensive technique, that is, after I have dispatched the attacker by blocking his attack and countering it.

I don't always put the pauses in the same place. If I do a kata five times in a row, I may pause in different places three of the times; sometimes I pause differently every time through. It just depends on how I feel.

I'll pause here to let the traditionalists scream.

7. NO HANDS PRACTICE

It's not uncommon for a kata performer to look better from the waist up. Because your arms are close to your eyes, you have a better sense of what they are doing and ensuring that they are doing it correctly. Your legs and hips, on the other hand, are further away making it a tad harder to detect errors.

Here is one way you can bring your lower body's participation in your kata up to par. It's fun and sort of weird, but after just a few workouts, you will notice an improvement in the rotation of your waist and hips, and a greater precision with your stances and kicks.

Forget your Arms

Stand in your ready position as you always do when beginning your kata. You aren't going to do anything with your arms during your entire performance except to let them hang down at your sides as if they were broken. From the beginning movement to the last one, use only your legs and hips as you perform the same footwork, same stances, same turns and the same kicks. Your hands and arms do nothing.

As you go through your kata in this fashion, you instantly become aware of your waist and hip actions and their important involvement in the delivery of power and speed to your hand and foot techniques. Usually after the second or third time through, you happily discover that you are putting more snap into your hip rotations, better form in your kicks and more depth in your stances.

Think of this as a body awareness exercise. Use this method whenever you feel the need to clarify the movements of your lower body.

8. USE YOUR EYES

A kata is a mock fight between you and a half dozen or more of your best enemies. As such, kata is a performance, a mini play in which you are the star the performer, the lead actor. As the star, it's necessary for you to emote, that is, express yourself, extend your energy and thus bring a sense of a real fight to your play.

Warrior Eyes

Exceptional actors emote with their eyes, and so should you in your mock fight. Your eyes should show all the strength, intensity and warrior spirit that is within you. It's mandatory that you see the imaginary attackers and pierce their flesh with your eyes. Someone once said about kata (actually, I think it was me), "Lead with your eyes, and your body will follow," meaning that your eyes need to create a sense of battle that your techniques translate.

Seeing is believing. Spark that imagination of yours and create a clear mental image in your mind of the attack that is coming at you. See the attacker's kick, see his punch and see your response. Feel your blow land and see him fall to the side. Snap your head in the direction of the next attacker and see him approach.

Seeing helps you maintain your psyche for the fight. The more psyche you possess, the more you put into your movements. The more you put into your movements, the more you progress physically, mentally and spiritually.

And the better fighter you become.

9. FLASHY KICKS

There are street fighting kicks and there are competition kicks; they are not the same. In a real fight, the best places to kick are below the ribs, targets that are easy to hit, hard to block and can be slammed with ultimate speed and power. Kicks to low targets are rarely pretty or exciting to watch, which means they may not be the best choice for tournament competition where the spectacular is judged higher than the practical.

"A person doesn't stand a chance if he is throwing fighting-type kicks," says Simon Rhee, a formerly regionally rated forms competitor. "The kick might be powerful enough to knock somebody down, but it has to look flashy, which in kata competition is what the judges and the audience are looking for, as opposed to hard and powerful moves."

Street vs. Competition Kicks

Know the difference between kicks for self-defense and kicks for show. How about a sidekick that thrusts straight up overhead into a vertical line? Where in the heck would you use that in the street? What would it do to your pants? And let's not even talk about doing a vertical sidekick while wearing a dress. Okay, the kick will work when you are lying on the ground and kicking up into the face of an attacker. But standing?

However, when a vertical sidekick is executed in kata competition, it looks impressive, it draws "ooo's" from the crowd and high marks from the judges.

How about those machine gun roundhouse kicks where the competitor turns in a circle popping out multiple high roundhouse kicks? When done well, this always gooses the crowd into manic cheering and dazzles the judges into awarding high points. And it should, since it demonstrates excellent form, strength and flexibility, some of the primary elements being judged in kata competition.

But would the machine gun roundhouse kicks work in the street? Can you really see yourself turning in a circle in one spot, nailing charging assailant after charging assailant in the nose with perfectly executed roundhouse kicks? You can? Well, let me tell you about this bridge I've got for sale . . .

Mixing High and Low Kicks

Kata competition is about expressing the art of karate. While it's okay to have three or four low kicks, you want to sprinkle your kata with flashy high ones to demonstrate your skill. If you do a low kick, do it to contrast a high one that follows. For example, snap a razor-sharp sidekick to an imaginary attacker's knee, pause for a half second, and then lean back and snap a head-high hook kick. The high kick is by itself impressive, but when it follows a low one, it looks even better.

Speed, power and control makes a high kick a winner. Speed and power means that the kick moves at tremendous velocity and looks as if it could knock out a horse. Control means that the competitor can execute high kicks *effortlessly*. He clearly doesn't have control when, because of a lack of flexibility and strength, he has to rely on momentum to "throw" his kick upward.

Training for High Kicks can Make you a Better Fighter

It takes disciplined effort to develop the necessary flexibility, strength and control to make high kicks look easy. My fighting style primarily kicks to the waist and lower, so when I competed in kata division I never fooled myself into thinking that my flashy high kicks were of any direct value to me in my job as a street cop. Indirectly, however, I benefitted from the extra flexibility, strength and control that my training for those kicks gave me. While I always trained hard to have fast and powerful low kicks, training my muscles for high kicks gave my lower ones even more power and speed.

A final note. If you are going to incorporate flashy kicks, they have to be executed with excellence. Many times I have judged tournaments and seen simple kata, with basic low and mid-level kicks, win over those with flashy kicks. This was because the competitor throwing those basic, low kicks was doing a better job of it than the competitor executing the high, flashy ones.

I remember a fellow judge challenging me as to why I gave a competitor low marks. "He did all those high kicks, and he did that somersault," the judge said, apparently believing that if a competitor *attempted* flashy moves he should automatically get high marks. "Why didn't you grade him higher?"

"'Cause he sucked at all those things," I said.

If you are going to use the flashy ones, develop them to perfection.

10. ON NOT WINNING

If you don't win a tournament, don't worry about it and don't let it get you down. Remember, you are trying to keep negative energy to a minimum. Tell yourself, "Hey, I can't win every time."

Don't even get me started on judges. Okay, I will. Sometimes you get a panel that is looking for a particular element that you aren't giving them. They like soft styles and you're a hard stylist. They like the somersault and cartwheel katas and yours is the meat and potatoes kind. I've won tournaments when I knew I shouldn't have, and I've lost when I was convinced my kata was the best. That is just the way it is.

You Learn More when you Lose

I don't think it's good for a competitor to win all the time, anyway. When you always win, you lose motivation and drive to train hard and compete hard. And most people who win don't analyze their performance as to how they can improve, because they are too busy feeling good and patting themselves on the back.

I entered twice as many tournaments as I won. I learned more from my losses because they forced me to evaluate, critique and make improvements. When I won, I just gloated.

5 ways

to Increase your Power

Before we get to the specific exercises that increase your power, let's review six important elements that you should now be incorporating into the execution of your techniques. If you have never learned these, shame on your instructor. If you know them but have let them slip your mind, begin using them again right now and enjoy an instantaneous increase in power.

Incorporate these elements, add the suggested exercises that follow into your workout, and you will soon be a walking explosive device. You may even be compelled to sign up with one of these phoney mail order businesses that register your hands as "deadly weapons."

1. SIX IMPORTANT ELEMENTS

Each of these elements by themselves will enhance your kick or punch with power. But when combined at the moment of impact, whether that impact be a board, an attacker's face, or a heavy bag, your power will be increased many times over.

Concentration

This is intense mental focus where all of your being is zeroed in on the moment, your technique and the target you are hitting. Nothing else exists. You are one with your technique. You are a missile streaking into the target with every ounce and fiber of your existence.

Mass

Let's define mass as the size and weight of your body. Though you may weigh only 140 pounds, it's possible for you to hit as if you were much heavier. Bruce Lee weighed about 135 pounds and it's said that he could hit as hard as a 225-pound man. The question is how do you increase your mass without porking out on cake and ice cream? By incorporating all the six elements listed here into your technique, especially speed.

Speed

I have a two-inch in diameter river rock lying here on my desk. If I toss it at your forehead at, say five mph, it will bounce off and maybe leave a little red mark. But if I throw it at 90 mph, it will put a dent in your forehead the size of a peanut butter jar. The mass of the rock didn't change and the striking surface of the rock didn't change, but the speed at which it hit you changed, and that makes the big difference. The next time you come to my house, I'll get my rock and prove it to you.

Reactionary Force

Sometimes this is called "opposite action." When you throw a punch with your right hand, there needs to be a simultaneous opposing action with your left hand. Your right punch goes out as your left snaps back to the side of your head or, if you are a traditionalist, to your left hip. The faster your reactionary force, the faster your punch.

When you throw a snap kick, the reactionary force is the fast return of your kicking leg. When you execute a thrust kick, your reactionary force comes from your upper-body motion. For example, when executing a sidekick your upper body leans quickly away from the direction of the force.

Concentrate on the reactionary force and watch your punches and kicks go out faster than ever before.

Breathing

I read a study on power lifting that said a sharp exhalation of air on the push portion of the lift can increase your power by 15 percent. This also happens in karate: Breathing out sharply adds to your punch or kick. Many times, new students are too self-conscious to exhale sharply, let alone grunt or shout. If this is you, you must get over it so as to take advantage of this instant power increase.

Balance

When your body is in balance, it's like a perfect chain in which every link is strong and doing its job. But if you over-twist, lean too far over your knee, wave your arms around or just simply stumble, you can't deliver all the power you are capable of because your unbalance has created a weak link. When your teacher talks about good form, he isn't talking about just looking pretty. Perfect form keeps you balanced and allows you to bring the other five elements listed here into play.

Examine all of your techniques to ensure that you are using all six of these elements in their execution. If you are not, and your technique is weak, well, that's probably why. If your techniques are strong in spite of the fact you are missing one or more of these elements, imagine how much more power you will have when you do the technique correctly.

2. MENTAL/PHYSICAL POWER LINK

Incorporating your mind into your physical technique will work wonders in the form of additional power and speed. There are many ways to do this, but because of space limitations, I have chosen one that my students like because they get immediate results.

The backfist is an excellent technique that far too many fighters simply snap out without consideration of its power potential. But it can be a powerful technique when you incorporate both the mental and physical, so powerful that it could easily break the neck of its victim. Here is a great method to link the two taught by Nisei Karate-do instructor Michael Holmes.

First the Physical

"To dramatically increase the power of the impact," Holmes teaches, "get some body weight behind the technique. This is commonly achieved in classical karate strikes by thrusting forward using big gestures and lunging steps. For beginners, this will emphasize the complete range of motions required to generate maximum power. Once this skill is acquired, you should practice the motion using shorter and shorter ranges until you are executing the backfist from a stationary stance. But even when not stepping forward, you can impart momentum of the body by incorporating it mentally into the final stages of the backfist."

Now the Mental

Here is how I incorporate this excellent advice. I think of the drill as "fooling" my backfist into believing that all 200 pounds of my body weight is behind it when I slam into the bag. To get to this point, I first break the drill into three phases.

Phase 1

Choose a method of stepping forward that is large and allows for a maximum momentum of your body weight. We use a step I call "crossover," which fairly describes the action. First assume a fighting stance with your left leg forward and with your hands up in your on-guard position. Your rear leg, your right one, slides forward, past your left and assumes a right leg forward stance. At the same moment that your right foot comes to a stop, execute a right-handed backfist into the bag.

Visualize your forward energy in your mind. For example, I see my image as being blurred as I streak forward from my left forward stance to my right forward stance. I *see* it happening, and I *feel* that thrusting energy.

Seeing and feeling this forward energy is the crux of this drill that you want absorbed into your brain so you can bring it out on demand.

Phase 2

This time, your lunge will be a shorter one. Assume a left leg forward stance with your hands in the on-guard position. Instead of taking the large crossover step, lunge forward with only your lead foot. First, launch your backfist, followed a split second later by a 12- to 36-inch lunge with your lead foot and a forward 10-inch scoot of your rear foot. Your backfist slams into the target just before your lead foot sets down.

Your thinking process is the same as in Phase 1. See and feel your energy explode forward. Don't think about the mechanics of the move, but occupy your mind only with visualizing that tremendous forward force. Although you step a shorter distance, see and feel the *same amount* of forward momentum energy as you did with the crossover step.

Phase 3

This time, don't move your feet forward at all. The only parts of you that physically move are your backfisting arm along with a slight forward inclination of your upper body. However, your mind moves forward. As you whip that backfist into the target, see and feel that same energy, that same momentum you saw and felt when you were actually moving forward physically.

If you have trouble bringing this forward energy into play, go back to Phase 1 and start over.

There is nothing mystical about this, but it does require mental concentration. I've had students hitting the bag at least one third harder 20 minutes after they learned the concept. I saw the difference in their movements, heard the louder smacks of their fists hitting the bags, and saw the big smiles on their faces when they realized they had accomplished something special. *(Mental note to self: implement an increase in students' monthly dues)*

See it, feel it and believe it, and you will be amazed at the increase in power your backfist can deliver without your taking a step.

3. REPS

I can hear you now, "Not reps agaaaaain, Christensen. You've already talked about the importance of doing reps several times in this book." Yes, I have and this probably won't be the last time. As I mentioned on the first occasion, if there is a secret to success in the martial arts, it can be found in doing repetitions, zillions of them.

My daughter can punch and kick with greater power than her appearance would indicate. She can slam into the hand-held pads so hard that it causes the holders to be concerned whether their arms will survive the experience. She is 18 years old as I write this, but she could hit hard even when she was 10. I know, because she doubled me over more than once with an errant and poorly controlled blow (as least she *said* it was an accident).

My point in bragging about my kid is this: She doesn't even remotely resemble Arnold Schwarzennergar. Physically, she looks like any other teenage girl. The difference, though, the one big thing that separates her from the other girls who spend the majority of their time watching MTV and gabbing on the phone, are the thousands upon thousands of reps she has pounded out since she began training at the age of five. While doing countless reps haven't given her bulging muscles, though she is as hard as a rock, they have given her a different kind of power. Some people might call it internal power, others, myself included, believe that her power comes from a conscious and an unconscious coordination of mind and muscle at the moment of impact.

Pushing to go Faster and Harder

Power also comes as a result of pushing your body and individual limbs to go faster and harder along a specific path. For example, when you repetitiously push your backfist to snap out faster, hit harder, and retract faster, you are rewarded, in time, with a fast and powerful backfist. The reps strengthen the muscles and the body learns to coordinate all its parts to make the blow a powerful one.

I have seen karate people, who have never touched a barbell in their lives, punch and kick many times harder than a person who can bench press 300 pounds but has never studied karate. Like I said, it's a different kind of power.

Here is the cherry on the pudding: If you perform thousands of reps using the many methods I have suggested in this book as well as ways you have learned elsewhere, and then add a couple of days each week of weight training, you will be one powerful fighter.

4. HEAVY BAG

The hanging heavy bag is sort of like a mirror: it reflects what it receives. If you're as ugly as a mud fence and stand before a mirror, it's going to reflect back ugly. If you have weak punches and kicks and hit the heavy bag, it's going to reflect those weak blows. You can't fool the mirror and you can't fool the heavy bag.

I mention this because I once heard of a "master" who had his students convinced, and probably himself, that his power was so incredible that his hits would barely move the heavy bag. Huh?

"My power is internal," he told his students in a sage-like voice. "My power goes so deeply into the bag that the bag doesn't move."

He probably tells them he can levitate, too, but not while they are watching.

The biggest mistake I see students do on the heavy bag is to train irregularly on it. Have you ever said to a fellow student, "I think I'll go hit the heavy bag for a while," you whack away on it for a few minutes, but don't hit it again for another two months? If you train with weights (and I hope you do), you would never say, "I think I'll go do some curls," do them for 20 minutes, but not again for another month. You know that for your biceps to progress in size and strength, you must do curls once or twice a week. That's called systematic training.

Train Systematically

To benefit from heavy bag work, you must also train systematically, at least once a week, twice at the most, with a routine designed for progress. If you train on it just once a week, I suggest you go all out and hit with full power. If you train on it twice a week, you should hit it at full power one workout, and then hit it at medium power on the second session. Most professional weight trainers use this approach, referring to as "heavy day/light day" workouts. They have found that by doing a lighter version of the same workout in the same week, they progress faster than when they go heavy for both workouts. Even knowledgeable, veteran trainers are discovering that they have been overtraining for years and by doing less they are starting to make gains again.

Train Regularly on the Same Techniques

How you hit the bag must be consistent, too. You can't do 50 reverse punches on the heavy bag on Monday and then not do them again for two weeks and expect to increase the power in your reverse punch. This is exactly how far too many students train. One session they backfist the bag to death and the next workout they slam it with roundhouse kicks. While this burns calories and gives you a good aerobic workout, it does little if anything to progress your hitting power with either technique.

Your workout has to be systematic and it must be consistent. The best way to ensure that you are doing this is to maintain a workout journal. Here is a basic heavy bag workout that uses all your primary muscle groups. Do the following on both sides.

Hand techniques	Kicks
Jabs - 3-5 sets of 15 reps	Front kicks - 3-5 sets, 15 reps
Punches - 3-5 sets, 15 reps	Roundhouse kicks - 3-5 sets, 15 reps
Backfists - 3-5 sets, 15 reps	Sidekicks - 3-5 sets, 15 reps
	Back kicks - 3-5 sets, 15 reps

These are foundation movements that will not only increase your power in the specific techniques, but increase power in other techniques that follow the same delivery path. Do this routine once or twice a week, and be sure to give yourself at least two days in between for rest. If you want to do, say, your ridgehand or your crescent kick in addition to this basic workout, go ahead. Just remember, in order to increase power in a technique, you must be consistent and you must train progressively.

5. WEIGHT TRAINING

Hopefully, supplementing martial arts training with weight training is no longer as controversial as it was back in the 1960's when opponent's warned, "Weight training will make you muscle bound." "It will make you slow." "It will restrict your movements and reduce your ability to flow smoothly from one technique to another."

There are people who believe that a fighter doesn't need to train with weights, since a perfectly delivered karate technique will have sufficient power to knock down an adversary. It's true that when a technique is physiologically correct, meaning every part of a fighter's body, from his toes to the top of his head, comes into play, the resulting force can be tremendous. In fact, this is the premise that the martial arts are based on; it's how a small fighter, after he has fine tuned his physical technique to perfection (I'm talking about reps again), can generate amazing power.

When all Things are Equal

When two fighters, let's make them green belts, are of equal strength, it's a safe bet that the fighter with superior technique and strategy will be victorious. But what happens when there are two green belts, who have had the same teacher, are equal in physical skill, experience, height, weight, and fighting smarts, but one has developed superior physical strength through proper weight training? I'm putting all my money on the weight-trained fighter. It's an easy bet for me because I have seen it over and over in my experience teaching martial arts since 1965: When two fighters have the same technical and tactical abilities, the stronger one usually dominates and wins the fight.

Stronger is Better

Let me be perfectly blunt here. If your instructor is telling you not to lift weights because it will make you stiff and slow you down, he is wrong. If you have come to believe that weight training is detrimental to your karate training, you are wrong. There is no middle ground here. It's been proven over and over, both anecdotally and scientifically, that when weight training is done properly, it dramatically increases the effectiveness of martial arts techniques.

I'm not talking about developing the bloated biceps and pecs of a professional bodybuilder. In all likelihood that could produce results that inhibit your technique, speed and even reduce your power potential. It's important, therefore, that you seek out information as to how to train specifically to increase power in your punches, kicks and blocks without creating a muscular physique that is detrimental to movement. On that note, allow me to give a shameless plug for my book *Fighting Power: How to Develop Explosive Punches, Kicks,*

Blocks, and Grappling.

The Four Tiers of Training

Think of your martial arts training as four-tiered, each one vitally important to your fighting skill and your ability to deliver awesome power. While each tier is important to the overall structure, it won't survive if it doesn't have a strong foundation.

Physical Preparation

The bottom tier is the foundation of your martial arts training - your power, speed, flexibility, balance, endurance, coordination and agility. Without any one of these factors present, without this quality foundation, the next tier will be shaky, progress will be impossible and your ability to execute effective blocks and attacks will be nil.

Technical Preparation

The more you practice, the better your technique. The better your technique, the greater your power that builds from the power from the Physical Preparation tier. See how each tier is important to the next one?

Tactics

The third tier consists of effective tactics. This is where you develop strategy to get your punches and kicks into the target and create a solid defense against your opponent's attacks. If your base tier is weak, so will be your tactics.

Psychological Preparation

The top of the pyramid is your psychological preparation for school sparring, tournament competition and street self-defense. But no matter how mentally prepared you are, it won't do you a heck of a lot of good unless the rest of the pyramid is supportive, especially the base.

Each tier supports the one above it and all depend on a strong foundation. When a good, result-producing weight training program is part of that bottom tier, all the elements in the other three tiers fall into place easily.

If you have time for only two weight training exercises, do the following foundation builders. The bench press works the upper half of the body and the leg exercises work the lower half. Not only will you gain power in your techniques, but you will look good in your bathing suit, too.

Bench Press

This is the mother of all exercises to develop power in your upper body. Many people think of it as only a chest exercise to build the pectoral muscles, which it does. But it also does a great job of building strength and power in the breast plate above your pecs, the front portion of your shoulders, neck, back, especially the upper lat (latisimus dorsi) muscles, arms, hands, wrists, and forearms.

Powerful chest and shoulders are important to your karate for at least three reasons. First, they act as the supercharged engine that drives your hand techniques. Try this: Extend your arm in a reverse punch and use your free hand to feel how your chest muscles bunch as your arm moves outward. If those same muscles can bench press a loaded barbell, imagine how much more power your reverse punch will have.

Secondly, a scrawny, bird chest will collapse when that assailant's big hairy fist or a competitor's uncontrolled kick slams into it. Use bench presses to build a cushion of muscle on your chest so that you can better absorb impact (but keep working on your blocks, too).

Lastly, a thick-looking chest may have a psychological effect on a bully and deter him from picking on you. If you were the street punk, would you target that thickly muscled guy or that scrawny guy?

Bench presses stimulate your neck muscles, too, and a strong-looking one can have the same psychological deterrent on some bullies that a strong chest does. But even more importantly, a strong neck helps you stay awake when you eat an unblocked punch to your face. Unconsciousness from a head blow is usually caused by the brain banging against the skull. The stronger your neck, the less brain banging and the more awake you will be to defend yourself.

As you press the barbell upward, notice that the motion resembles the straight punch. This means that you are using the exact muscles bench pressing as you do reverse punching or pushing someone away from you. It doesn't get much better than that.

Indirectly, your backfist strike is also getting some benefit from the bench press. Besides the chest, the exercise works the triceps, that three-headed muscle on the back of your arm that is involved in snapping out quick and powerful backfists. The bench press also stimulates the muscles around the elbow, which help to protect the joint from injuries that often occur from overextending the backfist and other punches.

I like to perform my bench press reps faster than most people do. I press up fast, though I never snap my elbows, and then I lower the bar twice as long as it took me to push it up. So, if I take one second to do the up motion, I take two to three seconds to lower it. If I were to push the bar up slowly every training session, I would develop bulk, especially when using heavy weights, but I wouldn't develop explosive speed. My way works the fast-twitch fibers, which develops the explosiveness I want in my hand techniques.

I lower the weight (called the eccentric movement) slowly to emphasize muscular tension, and then I rapidly raise the weight (called the concentric movement) to emphasize power and speed. To save my joints, I don't lock my elbows at the top.

There has been a lot of talk in weight training circles about doing only one set of an exercise and pushing the reps to failure. While this will make you strong, as well as put you at risk of injury, it actually reduces the rate of force production and speed, which is not what you want for your karate techniques. But when you divide the work into four or five sets of bench presses, which means less weight, you are able to perform each set explosively.

Do four or five sets of 10-15 reps once a week. More is not better.

One-Arm benches

This is a marvelous exercise that goes straight to heart of the reverse punch muscles. You probably won't develop the same overall upper-body power you do with the barbell benches since you are using fewer muscles and less weight, but the advantage of this method is that you are following the same tract with the single dumbbell that you use with the punch.

Lie on your back and grip a dumbbell with a weight that allows you to do about 15 reps. Position it along side your chest with your palm facing inward. Press the dumbbell straight up, rotating your hand as you do when you punch.

Oh yes, be sure to hold onto something with your free hand or the lopsided weight will cause you to fall off the side of the bench.

Do three sets of 12-15 reps, using the one second up and two to three seconds down count.

Weight Training for Legs

Here is a leg routine used by Instructor Frank Garza. He likes to hit his legs hard with unique karate drills and especially hard with weights. Here is how he trashes them with the iron pills.

"This is the leg workout I do twice a week," Garza says. "Depending on what I have going on, I might do two light workouts or, if I'm on vacation, I do two heavy workouts. Usually, I do a light workout if I have a class within 12 hours and a heavy workout when I have 48 hours of rest before my class.

Here is my light workout:"

Barbell Squats

Your warmup weight for 1 set, 8 slow reps. Stretch for two minutes. then . . .

. . . 80% of your maximum for 1 set, 10 to 15 reps. Focus on good form and get those muscles BURNING!

Leg Extensions

Your warmup weight for 1 set, 6 to 10 slow reps. Stretch for a minute and then . . .

. . . 80% of your maximum for 1 set, 10 to 15 reps. Focus on form and get those muscles to *burn baby burn*. Stretch for 1 to 3 minutes and then . . .

Leg Curls

Your warmup weight for 1 set, 6 to 15 slow reps. Stretch for 2 minutes and then . . .

. . . 80% of maximum weight for 1 set, 10 to 15 reps.

"On light workout days, make sure you get at least six hours of sleep before your karate workout.

This is my heavy workout:"

Barbell Squats

Your warm-up weight for 1 set, 10 to 15 slow reps. Then after a two minute rest . . .

. . . 80% of your maximum weight for 5 sets, 3 to 6 six reps. Stretch for three minutes between each set. When you can do more than 6 reps, increase the weight by 20 lbs. and do the reps more slowly.

Leg Curls

Warm-up weight for 1 set, 10 to 15 slow reps. Then after a 2 minute rest . . .

. . . 80% of your maximum weight for 5 sets, 4 to 6 reps. Be careful if your hamstrings tighten too much. Stretch for 3 minutes between sets.

Thigh Extensions

Your warm-up weight for 1 set 10 to 15 slow reps. Then after a 2 minute rest . . .

. . . 80% of your maximum weight for 5 sets, 3 to 5 reps. Rest and stretch for 3 minute between sets.

"Use the seated thigh extensions to test your pain threshold and your resolve to be your best," Garza recommends. "If you do the exercise correctly, the resultant burn will definitely test your pain threshold. If you are not feeling it, put more weight on . . . but keep in mind that form is more important than weight.

"Do a five to 10 minute stretching session at the end of your weight workout and make sure you get six to eight hours of rest each of the two days after your heavy session. Your muscles need this time to grow and get stronger."

Although it's extremely important to supplement your karate training with progressive strength exercises, you still need to train for precise fighting technique. I can cite many, many examples of weight-trained fighters dominating non-weight-trained fighters, but I can also relate stories of non-weight-trained fighters with superior technique beating the tar out of powerfully built fighters with poor fighting technique.

You need to have balance: excellent strength and excellent technique. Excellent technique will reward you with great power, and power training will make your excellent technique even better.

to Train for Self-Defense

Most schools teach karate techniques to use against other karate fighters. The reality is that the chance of you having to defend yourself against another person versed in karate is quite slim. Yet we all drill on ways to defend against sidekicks, hook kicks and charging ridgehand strikes, all techniques unique to the martial arts. So, are we really training for the street or just fooling ourselves?

I believe that karate vs. karate training is valid for self-defense, but it's important to understand how and why in order to have confidence in your ability. You are not only learning to defend against your fellow karate students, but you are also learning defense against various directions of force, whether that force comes at you in the precise form of a trained karate student's technique, or a drunk man's wild punch.

Although you may never see a perfectly executed ridgehand strike on the street, you will see a flailing roundhouse-type punch, a typical technique thrown by an untrained person that basically follows the same track as the karate ridgehand. By learning to block and counter the ridgehand, you also learn to defend against a street assailant's punch.

Often, basic karate techniques are easier to defend against than sloppily thrown street techniques. For example, when my class drills on a particular defense against a roundhouse kick, I point out that few untrained people are able to throw a circular kick as pretty as the karate roundhouse. Nonetheless, street fighters commonly throw circular-type kicks and, more times than not, they aim them at their victim's legs, a target that can be harder to defend against than a kick to the waist. Therefore, we first train to defend against 10 reps of our partner's nice karate roundhouse kicks, and then our partner deliberately throws 10 sloppy and erratic, low roundhouse kicks, mimicking what a typical untrained street assailant would do.

You shouldn't differentiate between self-defense training and all the other drills, exercises and training regimens you do. The two do overlap, although adjustments often have to be made since most street assailants use techniques that are not as clean as those used by your fellow karate students.

There are hundreds of exercises and drills that relate to street self-defense. Because of space limitations, I have chosen 10 exercises, drills and fighting concepts that have helped me survive some hairy confrontations. With some modification, many of them will apply to karate competition.

1. SIDE STEPPING DRILL

Whenever my instincts told me that a person was going to resist my arrest, I would lunge and grab hold of him, often startling him into submission. There were occasions when I got a person who scrambled backwards in an attempt to get away, but this never worked because I just continued my charge until he lost his balance and fell onto his back.

Far too many martial artists scramble backwards in response to a straight charge by an attacker. This works for a step or two, but when an attacker explodes forward driving you back more than three or four steps, the chance of you entangling your legs increases about 100 percent. It's a bad habit to do in a wide-open school, and it's especially a bad thing to do on the street where there are trash cans, fire hydrants (one day I will tell you about a fire hydrant that attacked my shin when I was wrestling a violent suspect off a city bus and onto the sidewalk), curbs, light poles and passing vehicles. When you back into any of those things, you potentially add another problem to your self-defense situation.

I attended a seminar once in which an outstanding jeet kune do stylist (sorry, I can't recall his name) demonstrated the inherent weakness of backing up. He charged several black belts, one at a time, bombarding them with hand techniques. To their chagrin, every red-faced black belt tripped and fell down, most after only three steps.

Move Out of the Path

One way to avoid getting your feet entangled is to sidestep out of the path of the linear charge. I remember at least two of the suspects I charged sidestepping, leaving me grabbing at empty space where they use to be. I don't know if they had trained to do it or it just happened by chance, but it sure worked.

Sidestepping is not as natural as scooting backwards, so it requires work to be skilled at it. Here is a sidestepping drill taught by Nisei Karate-do instructor, Michael Holmes that will help you make sidestepping a natural response.

A Good Drill

"One bad habit many martial artists acquire," Holmes says, "is to retreat rapidly when attacked. This is a serious tactical error. Using this drill will help to eliminate this bad habit for both self-defense, and for tournaments where backing out of the ring can get you warnings."

Holmes points out that when you step back, the attacker is usually too far out of range for you to hit with a counter. You may have avoided being struck, but you are no further ahead than you were before.

"This is a two-person drill," Holmes says, "that begins with your back to a solid wall, your rear heel 12 -18 inches from it. The attacker assumes a fighting stance facing you, and then attacks throwing an assortment of punches and kicks.

"With a solid wall behind your rear, you can only move sideways, diagonally or forward. Optimally, your sidestepping should intentionally leave you within striking range of the attacker. Sidestepping a large distance is not the goal, since it would not allow for counterstriking."

"The ideal response," Holmes says, "is to eliminate the attack by a pre-emptive strike [hitting the attacker before he begins his attack]. The next preferred response is a counterstrike to the attacker after sidestepping. A third option is to sidestep with a block and counterstrike combination. A fourth is to merely sidestep to safety without counterstriking.

"Ways to enhance the drill include altering stances to the less dominant side, or to use stances uncommon to you. Attacks and defenses should always be strong, realistic and a challenge to both of you. After each attack, you and the attacker resume your original starting position.

Begin with your back against a wall to prevent retreating.

As the attacker punches, sidestep quickly, and execute a strong counter.

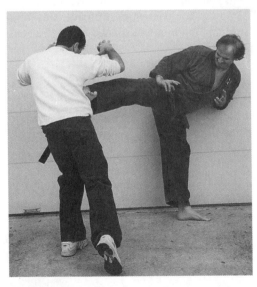

"Generally this should not be introduced to beginners, but rather to fighters with some experience. With time and practice, the sidestepping drill will produce a better fighter because the wall eliminates running backwards as an option."

2. TRAIN TO HIT FIRST

Allow me to toot my horn for a moment (hey, it's my book). Between my years as a military policeman in the army and my years as a city policeman in Portland, Oregon, I put in nearly three decades arresting people who didn't want to be arrested. In spite of this, I don't have even a little facial scar, a bent-over nose or even a cauliflower ear. I'm still blessed with the incredibly flawless face you see in the pictures. The reason? I never ever gave a bad guy the opportunity to catch me by surprise. I managed this by always catching him by surprise.

Do it Legally

But you have to be careful with this approach, because there is a fine line between defending yourself with an offensive move and simply assaulting someone. Before you charge into a guy, there needs to be some indication that he was about to throw a punch or in some other way do you harm. For example, a guy standing five feet away and calling you and your mother several derogatory names is not grounds for you to jump him. But if he takes one or two quick steps toward you, clenches his fists and spits out a threat that he is going to kick your butt, you are justified to take him out.

When you successfully strike first, you instantly establish psychological and physical intimidation. Notice I said "successfully strike." If you strike first and miss, you not only embarrass yourself, you give away your element of surprise, which means your next move will probably have to be a defensive one. Trust me on this: I've missed before, and was my face ever red. So how do you increase your success rate for offensive defense? By training.

Train to Beat your Partner to the Punch

Stand in front of your training partner in a natural standing position, as if you were standing on a corner waiting for a bus. Assuming your usual fighting stance would give away your intention, that is, even if you had time to get into a stance in an explosive street situation. But don't worry about not being in your fighting stance because after you have trained in a natural, standing position for a while, it will be just like another fighting stance to you.

From this position, determine what is your best technique for beating your partner to the punch. Your choice should be based on which of your techniques is fastest and closest, and leaves you in the best position to escape, deliver follow-up blows and to defend yourself should your surprise blow be blocked and countered.

Here is an example using a backfist. Begin by standing naturally, with your training partner in front of you about six feet away. When he clenches his fist and steps toward you, simply step forward and deliver a snapping backfist to the side of his head. It's quick, and since your body rotates slightly away, you are afforded some protection in the event he is quicker than you anticipated and able to launch his punch.

Create as many scenarios as your imagination allows and work out solutions for each one.

3. REFLEX TRAINING

There you are waiting for your bus, leaning against a light pole and sipping a latte (double shot with extra foam). Out of the blue, a punch, launched by an unseen person, slams into the side of your face, sending your gourmet coffee splashing across the sidewalk followed by your new bridgework.

No matter how that situation turns out, one thing for sure is that it will be a long time before you ever lean so casually and inattentively against another light pole. In fact, you will probably go about your day with high-strung nerves and eyes as wide and busy as a spooked deer's. While such anxiety may not be a healthy state of mind, a certain level of readiness is a good place to be whenever you are out and about in today's crazy world.

Sharp reflexes are absolutely mandatory for self-defense. Without them, you are just a walking heavy bag for anyone wanting to do a little bag work. The good news is that sharp reflexes are not hard to develop and they are even easier to maintain. But you do have to make the effort.

Random Attack Drill

Instructor Frank Garza is a strong advocate of reflex training and offers this advice: "A drill that I like to have my students perform is to have one opponent stand still while the other does some kind of random grab or attack. The defender is almost always surprised to see how clumsy he defends himself. This is one of those drills (like almost all drills) that needs to be performed often until it becomes imprinted into the subconscious. There are lots of variations, too. For instance, you can have the defender walk by the attacker who throws a surprise punch, or you can have the defender sitting when the attacker passes by and punches him"

Pause-Attack Drill

Here is a drill I use to progressively build reflexes. I have the class form two lines and face each other; one line attacks and the other defends. On my count, the attackers launch a lunging backfist, but instead of lunging the instant I call out the number, they have up to 20 seconds to throw the technique. They might do the backfist the instant I say the number, they might do it five seconds later, 10, 15 or 20 seconds later. The defenders know what is coming, but they don't know *when* it's coming. And that makes it a reflex drill.

After each line has performed 10 reps with the backfist, we change the technique to, say, the reverse punch and do it using the same 20-second window. The next time we might do the drill with a kick.

When I feel that both lines look good, I increase the difficulty. This time on my count, the attacking line throws a technique sometime within the 20 seconds, but the specific technique is not designated. They can throw anything they want, reverse punch, chop, sidekick, whatever. To add yet another level of difficulty, the defenders turn sideways and use their peripheral vision to respond to the attacks. Your reflexes will definitely be on edge after going through these drills.

Hey, just because you are jumpy and paranoid doesn't mean there aren't people really trying to get you.

4. MOVE TO YOUR OPPONENT'S WEAK SIDE

I define what is an attacker's weak side in two ways: The outside of his lead hand and whatever side I've injured.

Outside of his Lead Hand

Let's say the attacker is standing with his left side forward, which positions his left leg and left arm forward. The empty space to his left, which I refer to as the "outside of his lead hand" is the direction you want to move. That space is empty because once you block or check his lead hand toward the inside of his body, he has no other weapons in that space.

This is a good concept against an untrained street fighter, but not a particularly good one against a trained karate fighter or a trained boxer. The trained fighter has no trouble shifting his stance and/or using his feet in a variety of ways. The untrained fighter, however, will usually just stand there looking perplexed because you are no longer standing in front of him.

Let's say the untrained fighter throws a couple of lead, left jabs at you, a typical attack that untrained people learn from watching boxing matches on television. You respond with a quick block, jamming his arm inward across his body, and stepping 45 degrees into the empty space to his left. Let's see now, what shall you do? Slam a roundhouse kick into his chest? Yes, that worked nicely. How about a solid punch to his ribs? Cool, that got in easy. Should you toss in another roundhouse kick for good measure since you have so much time and this is starting to get really fun? Sure, here goes.

While this works like a charm against untrained fighters, don't completely rule it out against karate fighters. There is always a chance that you just might catch one sleeping.

Working against his Injured Side

I've mentioned elsewhere in this book that I'm trying to recuperate from a seriously injured right shoulder. I still train, but when I spar, I hook my right thumb in my belt so I won't reflexively snap it out and enter that red-hot pain zone. My daughter, who I have taught to always aim for an attacker's weakness, loves to whip roundhouse kicks toward my injured side. What a kid!

When your attacker is clearly injured, you want to work against that injury with extreme cruelty. If his right eye has been poked during an earlier exchange, throw lots of circular attacks - back fists, roundhouse kicks, roundhouse punches - from outside his field of vision into the right side of his head or body. If his left knee is hurt, bombard it with kicks.

When engaged in a self-defense situation, fairness doesn't exist. Do what you got to do to win.

Free Tip

There is an old samurai saying that goes: *When you break your arm in battle, hide it in your sleeve.* This means that if you wrench a finger or hyperextended your elbow, don't let on. Your attacker may have read this book, too.

Strategy Tip: Move Outside

When you have a choice, move to the outside of his lead hand.

See the counterattack possibilities?

5. KEEP HITTING

There are a lot of martial artists convinced that they are in possession of one-punch killing techniques. I don't know how people get into this frame of mind unless it comes from too much tournament-style sparring in their schools. Because they can sneak in a punch or kick and score a tag, they have developed confidence that their blow would have knocked down their opponent, maybe even knocked him out.

Maybe is the keyword here: Maybe the blow would have knocked the person out, but most likely it wouldn't have. It usually takes more than one hit to stop an assailant, even when you hit him with that killer technique of yours that has hurt your training partners on occasion.

When two people are engaged in a desperate fight, they are supercharged with adrenaline, which increases their physical strength and their ability to resist pain. I've had to fight guys even after they have been shot, and they still fought like maniacs. I know of two occasions where suspects had been shot in their hearts and they fought the officers for several seconds before they crumpled dead to the ground.

Those blows that make your training partner bend over and gasp, probably won't even slow down a hyped assailant who wants to rip off your face. I learned this the hard way in the mean streets of Saigon, Vietnam. My reverse punches and front kicks that made my instructor so proud back in the states, didn't have the effect in reality that I thought they would. I found that to end a fight quickly and to end it with me being the victor, I had to hit the attacker multiple times.

Of course it's quite possible to end a real fight with one blow. During a raid of a brothel in Saigon (I was on the police side, thank you), I hit an attacker in the heart and he collapsed unconscious. He was whisked away to the hospital and for several hours it was touch and go whether he would survive. He did, thank God.

More often, however, I've hit guys with full-power blows, only to have them give me a look of annoyance. I've also found this true with grappling techniques. I've applied joint locks in street situations - the same techniques that have been tortuous to my classmates - only to have the bad guys look at me with an expression of, "Just stop it. That doesn't hurt, anyway." But I've also had people yelp and scream at even the mildest wrist lock.

Since you never know what an attacker's reaction is going to be to a punch or kick, the solution is to hit him multiple times until the threat is over. Never depend on a single move, technique, or combination. Instead, expect that you will have to throw multiple blows to get the job done. In the streets, there are no referees to pull you apart and no time clock to save the day. There is only you and your techniques, how ever many it takes to get the job done.

Free Tip

The fight is over when your assailant stops or verbally tells you that he wants to give up. Don't continue to bombard him with blows after he is down or indicates to you that he wants to quit. Yes, he started it, but if you continue to rain blows on him after he has given up, you become the aggressor in the eyes of the law. It's not a good thing when you get arrested in spite of the fact that the guy attacked you. Control yourself, and throw only enough techniques to get the job done - and then stop.

6. DEFENDING AGAINST A BIG GUY

Let me start out with some sage advice: *Don't fight a big guy.*

That said, here are some things to do on those occasions when you can't run away or talk your way out of fighting someone much larger than you.

Stay out of Reach

Don't let him hit you with his big, hairy fists and definitely don't let him get hold of you. Stay mobile to keep him off balance and frustrated, and don't let him set himself prior to throwing a blow. That only makes him stronger.

Attack his Weapons

Continually move around him, and when he throws a punch, duck underneath and punch up into his upper arm or into his elbow joint. When he punches again, slip to the outside and smash a hammer blow into his triceps, his elbow, or both. If you have time to launch another attack before you back away, claw his face and eyes. If he throws a kick, bring your elbow down hard on his shin or knee cap. An elbow to the knee takes the fight out of even the toughest guy.

Go to his Vulnerable Areas

Forget about hitting him in the head with your fist; you have to commit too much for that. And forget those body shots that get points in tournaments, because they won't phase him. Think in terms of giving him acute shots of pain to vulnerable areas, such as his elbows, the muscles of his upper arms, eyes, shins and groin. Applying your power to highly vulnerable targets makes you stronger than you really are. Check out the following section.

7. GIVING ACUTE PAIN

You have probably studied in your school or read in martial arts books and magazine about so-called vulnerable targets. The teacher or writer often makes great claims (I'm being nice here and not calling them absurd claims) about the implications of hitting these targets. "Hit a guy here," says the expert, "and he will drop to the ground writhing in agony and die a few hours later."

Have you ever asked yourself *how* the expert knows this? If his knowledge is from practical experience, then why isn't he behind bars, since killing folks can get you in a lot of trouble? The fact is, he doesn't know for sure. He may think he's passing on the truth, or he just might be purposely hyping his teachings to a class full of uninformed students. In either case, he is passing on garbage and perpetuating misinformation.

If you have been training for a while, no doubt you have been hit in a few of these vulnerable targets, either by accident or because you were training full contact. While the impact hurt and may have sent you cartwheeling to the floor, you didn't die. You didn't even writhe. Does this mean the target is not that effective to hit? Maybe. Or maybe you just weren't hit with enough power when you were off balanced and vulnerable.

When I was a street cop and working a pretty tough area, I found that many of those so-called vulnerable targets weren't so vulnerable. In order to get through my day, I came up with a short list of my own that didn't require ideal circumstances to get the desired results. I chose targets that when struck, more times than not, caused such acute pain and/or debilitation, that the fighter gave up his will to continue. *Destroy his will and you will be victorious*, someone said.

There is no 100 Percent Guarantee

There are no absolute targets or techniques. Whenever I say that in a class, there is always some wise guy who says, "Oh yeah? Well, a bullet in the head will do the trick." Sorry Charlie, but that just ain't so. I saw two cases of people shot in the head - one person took five rounds - and they were still running around screaming and putting up a fuss. I repeat: There are few absolutes.

Strategy Tip: Attack his Weapons

Even the biggest guy will lose interest in punching after you have struck the tender inside of his arm a couple times.

Catch his six-foot-long leg and ram your elbow into that tender place where his thigh muscle connects to his knee.

My List

Hitting these targets works more times than not. When the blows are effective, the acuteness of the pain forces the fight out of the attacker as fast as air rushes from a punctured balloon. The more acute the pain, the more the attacker thinks about himself, which is better than him thinking about you.

Eyes

If you slam a reverse punch into an assailant's chest, it will hurt, maybe even knock him onto his back. But the probability of him continuing to fight is pretty good. If you snap your finger into his eye, however, his desire to continue with your little tiff diminishes in a quick hurry, because his thoughts are focused only on his throbbing, weeping socket.

Adam's Apple

A punch in an attacker's jaw might hurt, but it will probably hurt your hand, too. If we ever meet, remind me to show you my right hand where my little knuckle *used to be*. To avoid making the same error, lower your aim and punch him in the throat. That technique saved my bacon one night and left the guy crumpled on the sidewalk choking and wondering how he swallowed a Toyota pickup.

Nose

No, you are not going to drive his nose bone into his brain for the simple matter that it's not a bone; it's cartilage. That Old Wive's Tale has been going around forever. But a good punch or kick there will cause an attacker some acute eye tearing, vision loss and tremendous debilitating pain. His mind will be completely on the anguish radiating from the center of his face, not on you.

Elbow Joint

Blows to the elbow joint are acutely painful because there are so many nerves that surround them. When your attacker wads the front of your shirt with his hand, slap his elbow joint with your palm or strike it with your forearm. When he is on the ground, stomp it with your foot. The impact from any of these blows will cause excruciating pain that will radiate from his finger tips to his shoulder, and the nausea may make him lose his lunch. It's a guarantee that for a long time afterwards, he will think of you every time he bends his arm to scratch his head.

Ear

A lot of karate students have no idea how powerful a slap can be. My senior black belt, Gary Sussman, can slap a hand-held bag so hard that the impact sounds like a gunshot and spins the holder in his tracks. Imagine that same blow landing against an attacker's ear. I can tell you from experience that the pain from a hard punch, slap, or kick against the ear feels like a knife passing into the brain. It hurts like the dickens and it leaves that recipient going, "Huh?" for a long time.

Fingers and Back of Hand

Grab your attacker's fingers, bend them in any direction they are not supposed to go, and then chuckle at how he yelps like a kicked puppy. When he
is in his on-guard stance, snap your backfist knuckles against the back of his
hand. There isn't a lot of padding there and the pain can be quite debilitating,
causing the guy to yelp and draw his struck hand into his chest to comfort it
with his other.

You can also stomp on his fingers or the back of his hand after you have
knocked him down.

A hard stomp to the fingers
of this guy's support hand
will give him acute pain.

Solar Plexus

This little pocket of vital nerves lies just below your chest and just above your
stomach. A hard blow there, if the guy isn't wearing a heavy winter coat, will
knock the wind out of him and even cause him to vomit. My partner struck a guy
there once with his police baton, and the guy projectile vomited, which can be
a little startling when you aren't expecting it. It messes up your shoes, too.

Kidneys

These are located on both sides of your body near your lower back. A strong punch, knee, or kick to either one will cause excruciating pain almost on a par to getting hit in the groin. But don't waste your time hitting there if the assailant is wearing a heavy jacket.

Groin

Little explanation is needed with this target as both sexes are vulnerable to the acute, debilitating pain caused when it's struck. It can be a difficult target to hit, however, especially males who are naturally protective of the area. When hit, all of the recipient's attention is focused there and, stand back, he may he may even lose his lunch. Keep in mind that, incredible as it may seem, there are people who can tolerate a hit to the groin. I'll leave nicknaming these guys up to you.

Ankle Bone

That little protruding bone on the outside of the attacker's ankle is vulnerable to a sharp kick with a hard shoe. The pain is numbing and debilitating. If the attacker is lying on the ground and that protruding bone is right there looking at you, stomp on it and he will be slow to get up to continue his attack.

Top of the Foot and Toes

Everyone knows that the toes are sensitive. A good stomp will cause the attacker to release his grip on you and think only about the agony radiating from his little piggies. If that didn't do the trick, stomp with the edge of your shoe onto the meatless top portion of his foot. That really hurts, too.

There are many other vulnerable targets on the human body. In my experience, however, when the above targets are struck, there usually follows acute pain and debilitation, so much so, that the attacker can think of nothing else. When that happens, his fighting spirit is diminished, sometimes destroyed.

8. CHOP-KICKING

Several years ago, I befriended the former editor of *Karate Illustrated* magazine, Renardo Barden, who had moved to Portland to finish a novel. We used to fish for trout together in one of the many rivers in the Pacific Northwest, and he would tell me stories of martial artists he had met in his job. He was especially impressed over a kickboxer who was skilled at chopping his opponent's legs with his roundhouse kicks. The fighter told him that when the muscles in either the front or back of the upper leg were struck at an angle, it shocked the muscle fibers and debilitated the victim.

Thinking this was interesting, I chop-kicked a training partner's leg the next time we sparred and - wow!- both of his legs crumpled and he crashed to the floor (he was sort of mad about this, but that's another story). Although my kick was fairly controlled, it sure took the fight out of the guy. Since then, I have kicked others with it and every one of them dropped. I don't know if it's really shocking muscle fibers, but it definitely buckles the legs.

Instructor Frank Garza favors this kick and, in fact, had used it during a sparring session the night before I contacted him for his comments.

"It works great," he said. "I prefer to hit the back of the leg at an upward angle with my shin because it seems to send a shock all the way to the hip joint and tightens the tendon to the butt. A chop-kick can more easily penetrate the leg and therefore transmit shock to the muscles and bone. I have hit sparring partners, and I've hit people I was throwing out of a club where I working as a bouncer. All of them would start limping immediately and complaining of a pulled hamstring muscle. A downward strike to the back of the leg doesn't seem to have the same effect, probably because the upper leg is much more muscular than the lower leg.

"When striking the front of the leg, the quadriceps, I prefer to use a downward angle with a shin kick. It seems to me that the muscles are weakest near the knee. It's also an easier target to hit, and there is less chance of the kick being grabbed as is the case when kicking closer to the hip.

"It's interesting that even though we can condition our shins to take impact, it's much more difficult to condition our upper leg to take blows."

As I said, it's a common reaction for your kicked opponent to drop to the ground when struck at an angle in the thigh. Many of the guys I've hit with it couldn't continue sparring because of severe cramping or an intense weakness in the limb.

Technique: Chop-Kick

Chopping downward against the thigh requires that you chamber a little higher than with regular roundhouse kicks, and then kicking with your shin at a downward angle.

The angle of the blow often creates a shock that causes your opponent's leg to buckle.

Another reaction is for the recipient to bend over at the waist and lift the struck leg in an attempt to protect it. He hasn't fallen to the ground, but he is virtually helpless and may be even hopping around on one leg. If you get a hopper, consider chop-kicking his support leg. Hey, make life miserable for the guy and he might think twice about trying to hurt someone else.

There is a remote possibility that you will get a reaction that takes you by surprise. Sometime you kick a guy with all that you have, and he just looks at you as if you didn't do anything. This is rare, but there are people who don't feel pain the same way you and I do. If you meet up with one of these guys, switch to other techniques, including whacking him in the head with a trash can.

9. THE FRONT KICK OFFENSE/DEFENSE

As a defense weapon, you can use the front kick with either the front leg or the rear leg, the front being quicker but the rear being more powerful. Muay Thai fighters usually consider kicking with the front leg as purely defensive, while front kicking with the rear leg as mostly offensive.

I suggest that you don't limit yourself to such absolutes in fighting. For example, since a good offense is a good defense, let's look at how doing the front kick with either leg can be used to stop an attacker's punch or kick.

Kicking with the Front Leg

Think of using the front leg as a boxer uses his jab: to keep your attacker nervous and on the defensive, and as a way of stopping or jamming his assault. For example, as he moves threateningly toward you, thrust your front foot at his hip or his lead leg. While you may not hit with enough power with your front leg to seriously hurt your opponent, you can at least stop him and possibly stun him.

Maintaining your balance during the kick is critical. Launch the kick with speed and then quickly snap it back to the ground to avoid having the attacker's forward momentum knock you off balance. It's also important to ensure that your energy is directed forward. If you lean too far back, which means your energy is moving away from the target, you risk being knocked off balance.

Consider this scenario. You find yourself face-to-face with a big lug who is threatening to make your head lonesome for your shoulders. You step back in an attempt to get out of range, but he follows with clenched fists and words that make it clear he is going to hit you. Since you don't want to wait for him to attack first, front kick his closest hip with your front foot, ideally a couple inches below his belt line. This *should* stop his forward momentum and give you a moment to turn and run or to follow-up with other blows. Front kicking his closest knee is more difficult because it's a small target to hit when under stress. But if you can do it, the impact might hurt him and possibly hyperextend his leg.

Rear Leg Front Kick

There is tremendous power potential when front kicking with the rear leg, because you can drive hard with your hips and penetrate deeply in the last three or four inches when your leg and hip is at total thrust. You can lean back, but not too far because you want your energy moving forward and into the target.

Let's say the attacker moves toward you and picks up his rear leg to deliver what will probably be a sloppy roundhouse-type kick. You must act the instant you detect his foot leave the floor because if you wait until he rotates his hip, you may be too late. As quick as a wink, thrust your rear front kick straight into his lower abdomen, front hip or lower thigh. Hit with the ball of your foot as your hips thrust forward and lean your upper body back slightly. You have to be fast to make this work, but you have some advantage since you are throwing a straight-line kick and he is throwing a circular one.

Choosing the Best Leg

Against a cocked fist, consider using your front leg since it's faster and closer to the assailant. If the attacker is especially slow or drunk, you might have enough time to use your rear leg; it's your decision given the circumstances. In either case, lean back as you thrust your kick to avoid his punch. Just be sure not to lean back so far that your kick is weak or you lose your balance.

More on Excessive Leaning

I've warned you a couple times against excessive leaning because it's a common error that gets a lot of fighters into trouble. I've seen students do it on the heavy bag, only to find themselves lying on the floor with red faces and a sore butt. I've also seen people do it when sparring and I've seen them do it in real fights. When you fall in school because of your own kick, you only get embarrassed, but falling in the street in front of your still-standing assailant can be quite dangerous.

Find that happy point where you lean back far enough to maximize your power and avoid getting hit by the attacker, but not so far that your energy is moving away from the target.

10. KNOCKING OUT THE ATTACKER

One time my partner and I got a radio call on an armed robbery at a nearby 7-11. A few seconds after dispatch told us that the suspect was 22 years old, blond haired and wearing a buckskin jacket, an old beater of a car passed through our intersection with a driver matching the description.

He pulled over quickly enough when we turned on our flashing lights, but then he leaped from his car and promptly punched my partner in his face. The suspect hit him with two more punches, knocking him against the hood of our car, and then he spun around and charged me. I blocked his first punch, and after blocking his second, I decided enough was enough. I slammed a reverse punch into his cheekbone (a move that broke my hand on another occasion, though this time I didn't feel a thing), knocking the guy into my partner who was draped over our fender rubbing his jaw. They both fell to the street, the unconscious suspect on top of my wiggling and arm-flailing partner (I remember thinking that my ol' pard looked like an struggling, overturned turtle).

After we got the slowly-awakening and profusely bleeding suspect into the back seat of our car, we drove to the 7-11 store to have the clerk identify him as the hold-up man.

"No," she said, trembling, as I held the groggy man up by his blood-matted hair, "that's not him."

Woops. I knocked out the wrong guy.

A quick end to the story is that we charged the guy for assault and tossed him in the clinker. He sued me for a $1,000,000 for knocking him out and breaking his cheekbone, but luckily the case was dropped when he went to prison a few months later for an unrelated crime, one that he really did do.

Knocking an assailant out isn't that hard to do as long as all the right elements are in place. It doesn't require tremendous power - I didn't hit the "holdup" guy with my best punch - but it does require accuracy. It also requires surprise. If your attacker sees it coming, he can tense his neck and face muscles and solidify his stance. The more solid these things are, the less trauma to his brain.

Play with his Brain

So, how can you take an assailant by surprise if he is standing directly in front of you watching your every move as he sets you up for attack? You have to manipulate his brain by saying something that will ever-so-briefly occupy his thought process and lower his mental readiness. Here are a couple of examples that may seem a bit silly, but that is the idea.

"What are you lookin' at, punk?" says the bully. "I'm gonna knock your head off." He gives you his big glare and waits for you to shake and sweat and stammer and swallow hard.

"Is that your car over there?" you ask, looking over his shoulder. Whether he looks in the direction of his car is irrelevant, though it's better if he does. What is important is that your question is immediately followed by your fist slamming against his jaw line. The idea here is to engage his mind in thought so that he is momentarily distracted.

"I'm going to kick your butt, sissy boy," another assailant says, glaring hard into your eyes.

"I'm sorry," you reply, with a puzzled look. "I didn't hear you." As he begins to repeat his threat, you smash your fist into his face.

When his mind is engaged in processing your question, even for a second, he can't react to your attack. His eyes have to first see your fist, the message must register in his brain, and his brain must send a response to his body. Although this happens quickly, it's enough time for you to successfully get in your punch.

Jar his Brain

When I punched the holdup suspect, my blow broke his cheekbone. This is not the usual knockout point, though it sure worked on him. The usual place is anywhere along the jaw line from the ear to the point of the chin. The closer to the chin, the quicker the knockout and the longer the recipient is unconscious due to brain trauma. Blows delivered closer to the ear shock the brain less, resulting in a shorter period of unconsciousness.

Put your weight behind your punch. Usually, the strongest blow comes from your rear hand, although your lead should be strong enough if you train it. Focus on the small target and drive your fist *through* his jaw using speed, arm power and body momentum. If all the elements are present, he should crash to the floor with little birdies flying about his head. If some of the elements are missing or weak, he may stagger back or fall to the floor for a second before he regains his feet. In either case, run away and call the police.

Some Important Things to Think About

Considering the inherent risk involved when a person's brain is jarred so severely, knocking out an assailant is a serious act. Additionally, because it's your punch that knocked the person out, no matter what the circumstances of the fight, you are responsible, at least to some degree, when his head hits an object or hits the floor so hard that further injury is incurred. I mention these two points because we live in a sue happy society, and things can get so twisted around in the justice system that you just might find yourself in big trouble. Be clear in your mind that the situation justifies such a level of force.

I've mentioned in this book that I'm not in favor of punching a person's jaw with a fist, since it's not much different than ramming your fist into a horseshoe. I've broken my hand doing it, and I know of others who have as well. Since I've never used my palm to strike someone in the jaw with the intention of knocking them out, I can't speak from experience as to the results. My guess is that it would do the job.

If you choose to punch someone's jawbone, know that you do so at great risk.

Remember that we live in a sue-happy society. If you go for a knock out or even a knock down, you may be held liable for any injury your attacker receives when he falls. Be sure your actions are justified.

to Prepare for a Belt Test

Ah, yes, the belt test. You love 'em, you hate 'em, but mostly you hate 'em. I'm not going to get into the debate here of whether there should even be belt tests. Instead, I'm going to proceed on the assumption that most martial arts schools have them, and that they are going to be around for a long time.

At first blush, *5 Ways to Prepare for a Belt Test* may not seem to fit into the theme of this book, which is how to fight better. But training for a belt test will ultimately help you. If you routinely train hard, an upcoming belt test nudges you to train even harder. And if you are normally a lazy trainer, a belt test will give you the shot in the arm you need to get moving. In either case, the end result is that you improve and rise to a higher level of skill. That helps you to fight better.

Some students shine during testing, while others fall apart and forget everything or several important things that only a week earlier they were doing competently. Here are five ways that worked for me when I was preparing for tests, and that I now teach my students to help them prepare for that big day.

When I began writing this book, my daughter, Amy, and my senior brown belt, Mark, were training hard for their black belt tests. They began a 16-week training program that was probably many times harder than the four-hour belt test. And that is the way it should be. *Train hard so the test will be easy* goes one axiom. Another I like is *Sweat in the school so you won't bleed in the street.*

Here are some training methods that Amy and Mark used so successfully.

1. KNOW YOUR MATERIAL

I don't know how many times students have come up to me a week before their test and asked, "I just read in my binder that I have to make up and demonstrate 10 combinations for part of my test next week. Do I really have to do that?"

I always answer them with a yes and no. "Yes you have to do that for the test, but no, it won't be next week, since there is no way you can prepare the combinations in time to be tested. Let's try it again next month."

Know your material, all of it. If your instructor doesn't have it all written down somewhere, then it's your responsibility to find out what you need to practice. If there is small print, know and understand it.

For green belt, my students have a written assignment as part of their test. One time a student took the test and passed it with flying colors. When I asked him for the written portion he asked, "Written assignment? What written assignment?" Admittedly, the requirement is a little hidden in the text on the sheet that lists the green belt material. Nonetheless, it's there and he should have seen it. I kept his belt until he brought in the written assignment the following week.

If kata is part of your test, ensure that you know every move and understand what each one represents. Understand the mechanics of all your sparring combinations as well as your single techniques. Know how a kick with your front leg is different than one with your rear leg. Understand the differences between thrust and snap, step and lunge, soft and hard. Be able to execute your kata and sparring techniques without thought and as hard as you can without error.

Tests are stressful events (so is a real fight), so make sure your material is imbedded in your mind.

2. PLAN FOR ERRORS

Stress and nervousness can play cruel tricks on you. Plan for them. Let's say you have to demonstrate several prearrange attacks, blocks and counterattack techniques with an opponent. During practice, you occasionally step too far, you miss a block or you end up in the wrong position to do your final punch or kick. Although errors are inevitable, it's important you handle them properly.

I almost always give credit to a student when he fills in a missed technique with something else, as long as it addresses the situation, and then I give him another chance to do it right. But if a student misses a move and freezes, I grade him down since it's obvious he is only responding from memorization and can't think for himself. Fighting is about improvising, so when a student errs and instantly comes up with a replacement, I know he understands what he is doing.

If the attack calls for your partner to punch high, but he punches low instead, you should still be able to block it and do the appropriate follow-up. How do you do that? By planning for it in your practice sessions. Know your test so well that when a screw-up happens, you can easily go with the flow and come out of it looking good.

215

3. KNOW WHAT YOUR INSTRUCTOR WANTS

I remember my mother asking me one time why I did so poorly on a high school history test. "'Uh, 'cause the teacher didn't ask me anything that I know," I told her.

Many of your belt tests won't examine your best techniques. Your instructor tells you that the test is on Kata One and you think, "Oh man, Kata Two is my best." Or, maybe you are a great kicker, but for green belt, the examination is mostly on your hand techniques. No test can examine everything, so there is a good chance that you will be tested on things that are not your best. So what do you do?

Look at the Bright Side

First, think of it as a positive thing, not a negative. When a test asks you to demonstrate material in which you are weak, think of it as an opportunity to improve. Let's say your kata is lagging because you hate practicing it, but since it's on the test, now you have to. You might not like having to do it, but in the end, when you are wearing that new belt and whipping that kata out like it's no big deal, you will be proud of your accomplishment. Think positively.

Train Hard on Everything

Just because you don't like doing a particular thing, doesn't mean your teacher won't test you on it. Life doesn't always go the way you want it to, and neither does karate training. Besides, the requirements are in the examination for a reason: They are important elements of the big picture that is your development.

If your instructor thinks as I do, and he knows that you don't like a particular aspect of your training or that you are having trouble with a particular phase, he will emphasize that during your test. I don't do this because I'm cruel (well . . .), but because I want the student to face himself and have to do whatever it takes to get the material ready for the test.

4. INCREASE TRAINING GRADUALLY

You might get away with cramming for your math test (though you won't retain much of your learning), but it doesn't work for a karate test. Your body will reject your attempt to cram by getting sick or injured, since cramming involves overtraining, something your body hates.

When Amy and Mark began training hard for their black belt exam, they designed a 16-week schedule that led up to the big day. Using material from the test, they *progressively trained* to improve their speed, explosiveness, power, flow and cardiovascular fitness. Although each week they pushed themselves a little harder, their bodies were able to handle it because their program was designed for growth. Since it was progressive, they didn't feel the strain they would have if they had waited until the last month to prepare. Additionally, they became psyched by seeing and feeling their skill and fitness level improve each week. Again, they wouldn't have experienced this within themselves if they had trained sporadically or had crammed the last three or four weeks.

Most importantly, they retained their skill afterwards because they trained progressively. If they had crammed for it, and somehow survived physically without overtraining, their skill level would have faded quickly after their test.

Rehearse

About three or four weeks out, they went through the entire test, just as if they were performing before the panel. They did this to check their cardiovascular fitness - the test was nearly four hours long of nonstop techniques - and to get a general feel, both physically and mentally, of going through the test in its entirety. Since the mental and physical strain was comparable to running a marathon, I suggested to them that they only go through it once before the actual test.

If your test is as long and strenuous as their black belt test and you want to do go through it more than once, do it once at about the 12-week-out mark, and again at about six weeks out. Following these rehearsals, train lightly for a week to give your body a chance to recuperate. Mark and Amy felt horrible for several days after their test. Be kind to your body and it will reward you many times over.

5. MENTAL REHEARSAL AND AFFIRMATION

Your body isn't the only thing you need to get ready for the big day. It's equally important that you program your mind to be prepared, to stay calm, to be confident and to do your best.

Be sure to read the section that follows called *Mental Imagery*. Use the techniques described there to prepare your mind and your emotional state in the following ways.

- To be relaxed
- To see yourself performing flawlessly
- To move effortlessly
- To see yourself in control
- To think that the test will be easy
- To see yourself courageous
- To see yourself confident
- To see that new belt wrapped around your waist

Whether you like it or not, the belt test is an inevitable part of your martial arts training. You can either let fear, anxiety and dread consume you and affect your performance negatively, or you can do all the right things to not only prepare and pass your test with flying colors, but to grow as a martial artist, in the process.

to Improve your Health & Fitness

When you have knowledge of the martial arts and know how to train, you are like a health club with legs. If something comes up in your life and you can't make it to your martial arts school, you can train almost any place without the use of special equipment. If you train smart, meaning that you pace yourself and train systematically, you can progress on your own without a training partner for months. And since martial arts training is so all inclusive as an exercise, you can work your entire body in just a few minutes.

Normalize your Weight

When done correctly and with the right eating habits, karate training helps normalize your body weight, helps you gain solid tissue if you are underweight and lose body fat if you have been downing too many cheeseburgers. It's estimated that a hard karate workout will burn about 600 calories per hour, which puts it right at the top of the activity list for calorie consumption. When you burn 3,500 calories you loose one pound. So, if you train hard three times a week, you drop about one pound every two weeks as long as your calorie consumption remains the same. If you reduce your calories a little, you lose even more.

Not a bad deal: You turn into a hardbody, and learn to defend yourself at the same time.

Great for Women

Many personal trainers recommend martial arts to women because it strengthens and firms the lower abdomen, hips and inner thighs, areas that when conditioned produce a youthful, feminine figure. After childbirth, these areas are usually stretched and weakened. Martial arts training will quickly restore muscle tone and health, and improve appearance.

Condition your Heart and Lungs

You can easily use martial arts training to work your cardiovascular system - heart and lungs - which provides you with some of the following benefits.

- Improves efficiency of your heart and lungs.
- Lowers blood pressure
- Increases blood supply, especially red blood cells and hemoglobin.
- Makes body tissue healthier as it gets more oxygen.
- Conditions heart
- Promotes better sleep.

A Good Cross-training Activity

If the martial arts aren't your only sport activity, you will happily discover that karate training will provide you with many benefits for other physical activities.

- Muscular strength
- Physical agility
- Increased peripheral vision
- Improved concentration
- Overall knowledge of your body

- Great energy
- Overall body speed
- Overall flexibility
- Discipline

It doesn't get much better than this. Karate training improves your body weight, mental concentration, reflexes, physical strength, flexibility, aerobic conditioning and provides you with a greater overall understanding of what your body can and cannot do. It seems like I'm leaving something out, though, but it's slipped my mind.

Oh yes, you also learn how to defend yourself.

Here are 10 ways to improve your health and fitness, which not only improves your fighting ability, but will keep you training for many happy years.

1. HOW TO DROP A FEW POUNDS

Sadly, we are an overweight nation and, even more sadly, is the fact there are far too many overweight martial artists stretching the seams of their uniforms. And when that overweight martial artist is an instructor - shame on him or her.

There are dozens of fad diets and exercise regimens on the market, and you have no doubt seen those late-night info commercials where they scam their way into your wallet. "Lose 10 pounds a week while gorging on cakes and pies," they lie to you. "Build awesome stomach muscles in only three minutes a day!" Hopefully, you know that these claims are all nonsense. There is no fast way to drop weight and do it healthily. *Fast* weight loss means you lost lots of muscle, which is not a good thing for a fighter.

Is there a good way to trim off those excess pounds without suffering hunger and losing muscle? Is there a way to keep it off? Yes there is.

This is what I did recently to trim off a few pounds. It's not a fad, gimmick or some extreme discipline that you can't maintain. It's an easy life-style and, what is really important to you as a hard-training martial artist, it leaves you with your muscle mass (actually, it can even increase it), tons of energy, and it will even improve your fighting ability.

I got the basis for this from the teachings of Bill Phillips, Editor-in-Chief of *Muscle Media* magazine. While his approach is primarily for bodybuilders, I modified it a little so that it fits the needs of a karate student.

If you hate rules, you will like the five that follow because they are easy to obey. Be obedient to them and you will enjoy watching your love handles melt away as you maintain your valuable muscles and improve your karate. Here are Bill Phillip's rules for weight loss with my modifications for the martial artist.

Rule 1

Do 20 to 30 minutes of aerobics three times a week, first thing in the morning on an empty stomach, and don't eat anything afterwards for one hour. Since you haven't eaten carbohydrates for several hours, your body get its energy for your aerobic workout from the fat in your body.

Throwing punches and kicks is hard for me to do right after getting out of bed, so I begin the regimen with a super fast 10-minute walk in my neighborhood. I find this to be easier on the joints and a great way to get an overall body warmup. When I get back, I immediately do 10 minutes of fast shadow boxing or fast combinations, periodically checking to ensure that my heart rate is between 75-85 percent of my maximum. That's all there is to it, except for the shower.

Rule 2

Lift weights. Do whatever weight routine you like, as long as you lift. The more muscle you have, the more calories your body burns, even when you are just sitting there looking out the window.

Rule 3

When you eat, take in about 10 calories per pound of your bodyweight divided into six meals a day. So, if you weigh 200 pounds, you should eat about 2000 calories a day (10 X 200= 2,000), spread over six meals of about 300 - 400 calories a meal. Trust me: You won't be hungry, especially if you eat a lot of protein.

Rule 4

Bill Phillips recommends one gram of protein and one gram of carbohydrate per pound of bodyweight, with 30 - 40 grams of fat a day. That is 200 grams of protein for that same 200-pound person. I find a gram per pound too much, so I only take in about ½ to 3/4 gram per pound of my bodyweight. Experiment to see what works for your body.

Rule 5

Drink a river of water. Knock back a 16-oz bottle of water upon awakening and keep a container at your side all day. Since both coffee and creatine, both of which I discuss in a moment, drain water from your system, drink a couple extra cups of water for every cup of coffee you have, and drink at least 16 oz with every five grams of creatine. Drink lots of water when you train and drink more when you are finished. Think of it as washing fat out of your body.

That's all there is to it. Make these easy-to-follow rules part of your life style and watch those ab muscles push their way through. And don't sweat it if you break a rule. Just make sure you get right back into the program the next day.

2. A FAST WAY TO AEROBIC CONDITIONING

I've used this training method for years but always in a haphazard manner without a specific system or a real understanding as to why it works so well. But it's been organized into a program now, one that works beautifully. Above, in #2, I mentioned Bill Phillips', magazine *Muscle Media*. Bill's brother, Shawn Phillips, is a contributing writer to the magazine and a guy with the most incredible abdominal muscles I've ever seen.

Shawn has developed a program he calls High-Intensity Interval Training. He uses jogging to teach the concept, but I'm going to show you how to do it using karate. It's an easy way (well, maybe not so easy) to get your cardiovascular system in shape fast, improve your speed and trim the ol' waist line.

The premise is simple: You shadow box for 30-seconds at moderate intensity, and then you go all out for 30 seconds. It's a lot harder than it sounds, but the good news is that you do it for only 15 minutes.

Burn Fat

With High-Intensity Interval Training, you burn fat more effectively than with low-intensity exercise, such as jogging; in fact, you burn up to 50 percent more efficiently. This easy-to-do program speeds up your metabolism and keeps it revved up for a while even after you have finished and hit the shower.

Get Faster

High-Intensity Interval Training also helps to develop your speed because during the all-out segments, you throw punches and kicks as fast as you can. Make the effort to push yourself to go faster each training session, and you will experience tremendous improvement in your speed.

Here is how you do it. After you have warmed up, begin by shadowboxing at medium speed for 30 seconds. At the 30-second mark, don't stop or even hesitate, but go all out for 30 seconds, throwing everything you have as fast as you can.

Do this Progressively

Even if you are in good shape, shadowbox for only four minutes using this method your first and second workout sessions. On your third workout, add another 30-seconds of shadowboxing at medium-speed, followed by a 30-second all-out session. Now you are doing the routine for five minutes.

Let's say you did your first workout on Monday, your second on Wednesday, and you added the fifth minute of shadowboxing on your third workout, Friday. On the following Monday, do another session at five minutes, and then on Wednesday increase to six. By adding a minute every third workout, it will take you eight weeks to reach 15-minutes.

At first blush this might look easy. But if you are giving that 30-second all-out phase all you've got, it will be a tough workout, one that will improve your speed, improve your wind, and burn calories.

3. SHOULD YOU TAKE CREATINE?

Everybody and their brother takes creatine these days, and for good reason: It works.

When I first began taking the stuff, I did an unscientific test to see if it made a difference in my strength. I chose an exercise in which I wasn't particularly strong - barbell shrugs. To do this exercise, you stand straight and tall and hold a barbell in front of your upper thighs. You then shrug your shoulders straight up, as if trying to touch your ears with them, and then slowly lower the weight. It's a great exercise to work the traps (trapezius) muscles that run along the top of your shoulders and into your neck.

I took 10 grams of creatine a day for the entire period of the experiment (the plastic scoops found in the containers of most brands hold five grams). In the beginning of the three-month period, I was lifting 70 pounds on my heaviest set (I told you I was a wienee). At the end of the three-month period, I was doing four to five sets with 240 pounds. I felt I could have gone even higher, but I was concerned I might get injured, since I hadn't strengthened other parts of my back as I had progressed in the shrugs. I increased in all my other lifts, too, but the shrug exercise is the only one I made special note of.

I still take 10 grams a day, five grams early in the day and the other five 30 minutes before my karate workout. If it's a weight training day, I take five grams before I lift and another five after.

A Shot of Energy

I've found that the creatine I take prior to karate practice gives me a boost of energy that carries me through the two-hour session. About half of my students take it, too, and report the same results. Some take it just before karate and others take it afterwards. They all claim they are stronger, and they enjoy a greater aerobic capacity for their karate training. Don't quote me on any of this because it's not a scientific study. It's just my experience with it.

Creatine is a compound that is made naturally in your body to supply energy to your muscles. It's technically called "methylguanido-acetic acid," which is hard to say if you just brushed your teeth. I'm not going into a scientific explanation as to how creatine works for two reasons. First I'm not a scientist. Secondly, it would take up too much space. There is a tremendous amount of information on the Internet, in magazines and in books on this relatively new supplement. Pursue those avenues if you are so inclined.

I'll conclude by encouraging you to try creatine. It's considered safe by scientists, doctors and sports medicine specialists. The only caution is that you drink lots of water when you are on it. In the last few years, the popularity of creatine supplementation has swept the country, and it's now used by body-builders to increase muscle size and power, and by runners and martial artists who want to make gains in power, speed and endurance.

4. WATER

As a hard training martial artist, you need to keep this thought in mind: By the time you feel thirsty, you're already dehydrated. When temperatures rise and your training session is hard and long, you must increase your intake of water to avoid dehydration. The warning signs are dizziness or lightheadedness, muscle cramps, nausea, headache, dark urine, sudden fatigue, and dry mouth and throat.

Not only are these symptoms signs of a health risk, they dramatically affect your training and progress. If your instructor is so strict that he won't allow you to take a sip of water periodically during your class, I suggest you find another school. If he is unaware of the health risk of not allowing students to keep themselves hydrated, you have to wonder in what other areas of your training is he ignorant.

Drink, Drink and Drink Some More

To stay well hydrated, drink 16 ounces of water two hours before your training session. One hour before you train, drink at least eight more ounces, and during your session, drink four ounces every 20 minutes. After your workout drink at least 16 ounces.

If you always drink from a water fountain, consider one swallow to be one ounce of water. If you have an especially small mouth or an especially big mouth (you know who you are), simply count how many sips it takes for you to empty an eight-ounce glass of water and use that number to determine your intake from a fountain.

Are Sports Drinks Better than Water?

Many martial artists prefer sports drinks over water because they taste better, and the good ones replace glucose and electrolytes, which are lost during your hard training. Whether you need a sports drink depends on your diet.

If you ate electrolyte-rich foods, such as, pasta, banana, chicken before your training, you should have plenty of electrolytes for about 60 minutes and, according to the American College of Sports Medicine, water is all you need. But if you train especially hard, in extreme heat and/or for longer than an hour, you begin losing more electrolytes than your body can spare - such as sodium and potassium, which fuels your heart and muscles. This is a good time for a sports drink because it will keep your blood sugar up, boost your energy and delay fatigue so that you can get through your hard workout.

Sports drinks that contain 6 percent or less of carbohydrates per eight-ounce serving will be absorbed fastest into your system. More than this will take longer to digest and may cause stomach problems. Also, the colder the drink, the faster it will be absorbed.

Try sports drinks, but read the labels and educate yourself as to which ones are effective and which are a complete waste of money.

5. VITAMINS C AND E

Since hard karate training depletes vitamins and minerals from your body, it's critical that you always get your daily requirements. Check out your local health food store for a quality brand that provides you with high potency.

About three years ago, after reading research as to how important vitamins C and E are to the health of hard training athletes, I began taking them in greater potency. Two months later, I happily discovered that my recuperation from hard training had improved and, after a year of taking them, I discovered I had had fewer sick days. For years, I had been getting colds virtually back to back, but once I began the larger doses of C and E, I had only one the entire year.

Little Warriors

Vitamins C and E are considered powerful antioxidants that make for a resistant immune system to fight off infectious diseases and illness. Your immune system suffers when you train hard in karate and when you restrict calories to drop a few pounds. These two vitamins helps you maintain a strong system that combats all those little critters that want to invade and make you ill.

How much should you take? I usually take two grams (2,000 milligrams) of C every day, more when I feel a cold coming on or I'm dragging from lack of sleep. I've gone as high as five to six grams when I've been sick; some people take up to 20 grams a day.

  The best vitamin C is the brand that is cheapest. Don't let anyone try to sell you an expensive formula or tell you that natural is better. Studies show that simple ascorbic acid works just as well as the expensive name brands. Just be sure to drink plenty of water when taking high dosages to reduce stress on your stomach.

I take around 800 IU of vitamin E, the d-alpha-tocopherol variety, every day. Some experts recommend as much as 1,200 to 1,500, though I have not experimented with such high dosages at this time. You should not exceed 1,500 since excessive E can be detrimental to your health.

Learn what dosages of all vitamins, especially C and E works best for you. You will be pleased with how you feel.

6. COFFEE: YES OR NO?

Will coffee help your karate training? Maybe, but you need to decide if it's worth it. I have used coffee for years to get a slight boost in energy for my workouts without harmful side effects. Other people, however, have problems since caffeine can make one's blood sugar level fluctuate, and because it contains acid that can cause heartburn and stomach problems during training. But not everyone experiences these problems. If you do, you have to decide if the energy kick is worth it.

In a study at Ball University, several athletes drank coffee without knowing it (how did they do that?), and every one of them found that their performance improved considerably; in particular, they were able to exercise 7 percent longer than without coffee. In another study published in the International Journal of Sports Nutrition, one group of athletes was given a placebo of glucose, and another group was given six mg. of caffeine per two pounds of each person's bodyweight. They were then tested as they cycled at different speeds. The end result showed that the caffeine group performed significantly better than the group that consumed glucose.

More is not Better

Studies show that two cups are optimum. One cup of coffee doesn't render the desired effect and three cups can be detrimental or, at the least, that third cup won't give you anything extra. We're talking about average supermarket cups, not those super-blast, Titanic-floating espressos that costs you five bucks.

It takes about 15 - 20 minutes for the coffee to get into your system and about 45 minutes for the total effect to hit. Therefore, you should drink it about an hour before you train.

New information is coming out all the time on the effects of coffee, and the preponderance of the findings shows that America's number one beverage is not all that bad for you. But keep in mind that it might not be good for *your* body so, as I suggested before, you have to experiment to see how you react to it.

Will java make you a better karate fighter if you are not one to experience its negative effects? Yes, it will indirectly, since coffee gives you an energy bump to train a little harder and a little longer, thus making you a little better.

7. SLEEP

As you may already be aware, hard martial arts training stresses your body, which is to say that it induces physical damage to varying degrees. It's while you are resting that the body rebuilds itself after all the tearing down you do punching and kicking. In oversimplified terms, overtraining occurs and injuries happen when you overwork your body but don't give it enough rest to rebuild. Quality sleep is the often overlooked anecdote to hard training.

Many experts say that hard-training athletes need at least eight hours of sleep per night. This is because sleep stimulates the release of growth hormones, an essential trigger for initiating muscle rebuilding and recovery.

Late Evening Training

You should know that the quality of your sleep can be affected when you train too late in the evening. Your body's metabolic rate, which is elevated during exercise, does not have time to return to its normal resting level. It's a low metabolic rate that gives you deep sleep. Also, intense exercise can alter your body's normal circadian rhythms (24-hour biological clock), which can affect how easily you fall asleep.

Many other things besides exercise can affect the quality of your slumber. For example, when you travel to a competition, it helps to keep your life as normal as possible so you get a good night's sleep. Avoid radical dietary changes, unnecessary naps, and changing your regular pre-sleep routine by watching late TV, reading too late, or socializing with other competitors. Try to establish a comfortable room temperature and bring along your own pillow.

Know that you may not sleep well the night before a competition, but also know that this restlessness has not been shown to hurt performance. At one tournament, I won three divisions and I hadn't slept one minute the night before.

While eight hours may the standard requirement, you might need nine, or you might require only six or seven. Finding the right balance of breakdown (training) and rebuilding (sleep) can make or break you as an athlete.

8. TAKE A BREAK FROM TRAINING

Frank Zane won the Mr. Olympia, bodybuilding's highest award, three times back in the 1970's. I had the honor of meeting him once and attending his seminar. Besides being a champion bodybuilder, one who brought a smaller, sleeker and more refined look to the sport when big and bulky was the norm, he is also a scholar and writer on all areas of fitness.

He believes strongly in the importance of taking time off occasionally to let your body, psych and spirit rest and recharge itself. When I was a young, hard charging bodybuilder, this was hard to do; in fact, I didn't do it. I couldn't, or at least I thought I couldn't. But during those times I went on vacation, I would force myself to only eat and sprawl by the pool. After a week or two of this, I was rested, my little aches and pains had dissipated, and I was spiritually and psychologically hungry to get back to the weights and karate training. When I resumed, I was happy to find that I hadn't lost a thing; in fact, my poundages increased and my karate techniques were sharper and faster. Now I take three or four days off every four months, and I always come back stronger, faster and more driven.

When you Can't Take Time Off

There is a way you can take a rest and still train at the same time. Let's say you have been going at it hard for several months, both in your school and at home. This body part hurts, so does that one, and it's getting harder and harder to get your rear in gear for the next training session. But for whatever reason - a pending competition or a belt test- now is not the time for you to take a break. Here is what you can do.

Occupy your thoughts with other things: baseball, movies, gardening, anything but karate. Think about your fighting art when you are in class, but the minute you leave, shift your mind to something else. And don't train at home. Okay, maybe a little stretching, but only while watching TV. If you normally train twice a week at your school and twice a week at home, reduce your training to only those times when you go to class, and then kick back and relax on those days you normally train by yourself.

Do this for three weeks, then resume your old schedule. By having just "gone through the motions" for a few weeks, you will feel like a million bucks and be physically and mentally charged to hit it hard again. And you will not have lost any of your hard-earned gains.

9. OVERTRAINING

One mistake far too many martial artist make, especially when starting out, is that they train excessively without getting sufficient rest. In recent years, study after study has shown that more is definitely not better when it comes to training. With weight lifting, for example, studies show that progress can be made with as little as one intense set per exercise (I discussed earlier why this approach is not a good idea for karate training).

Over the last few years in my weight training, I have gone from working each body part three times a week, to working each one two times a week, and for the last three years, one time a week. And even as a guy in his early 50's, I'm making progress. Sheesh! I wished I would have made this finding years ago.

Stimulate not Annihilate

Your objective when training, whether with weights or karate, is to stimulate your muscles, not annihilate them. Get out of the mindset that you haven't had a good workout unless you are crawling on your hands and knees out to the parking lot after class. This is an absolute fallacy that hurts far too many students. Your training should be vigorous, challenging, and brief with ample rest in between sessions.

It's not a good idea to *train hard* more than four days a week. There are times, however, when a tournament, belt exam or demonstration is coming up and you need to train five or six days a week. This is okay as long as you get plenty of sleep and good nutrition and you don't do it for an extended time, such as more than three weeks.

Leg day/Hand day

When Amy and Mark were training for their black belt examination, they began their 16-week countdown by training six days a week as if possessed. I didn't know they were going at this intensity until about the third or fourth week when I noticed they were showing symptoms of exhaustion. I knew they wouldn't listen if I told them not to train every day; they were just too driven and nervous not to. Instead, I suggested that they design their workouts so that one day their workout emphasized kicking and other footwork, and the next day they emphasized their hand techniques. They listened and immediately reported back to me that they had more energy.

Hard day/Easy day

One other device you can do is to alternate hard and easy training days. Say you are preparing to enter the kata division at an upcoming tournament. Since kata involves your entire body, my previous suggestion of having an arm day and a leg day doesn't apply. What does work is to have a hard training day followed by an easy training day.

I used hard day/easy day during the years I competed in kata and it worked every time. On hard days, I would push myself to improve my power, explosiveness and speed. To do this, I'd go through my kata over and over, which also conditioned my cardiovascular system. I needed to be aerobically fit since all of our katas contain 100 moves and invariably there would be a tie, meaning I had to go through it again.

On my easy days, I went through my forms slowly, ensuring that I was doing each move perfectly and that my transitions were smooth and effortless. Sometimes I did my kata to soft, gentle music, such as Japanese flute.

You are only Flesh and Bones

If you are driven to train several times a week, I compliment you on your desire. But you must train smart and not over do it. You might think you are a super hero (I hate to be the one to break this to you), but you aren't. As a mortal, made of flesh and bones, your body seeks revenge if you don't give it rest. Your knee will blow, or it might be your lower back. Most commonly, you lose your drive to train and begin to rationalize why you should skip class and sprawl on the couch.

Train hard, but get lots of rest, too.

10. MODERATION IN ALL THINGS

These four words will save you a lot of pain, ill health, money problems, training injuries, and relationship problems.

A central component to having balance in your life is to live in moderation. It's a simple concept: To stay healthy, you should eat nutritiously, exercise, sleep, and have time to yourself, but all in moderation.

Know that even the good things I've discussed in this section can be bad for you when taken to excess. As important as sleep is, if you get too much you feel groggy and sluggish all day. Take too much creatine, the miracle supplement I discussed earlier, and you might experience kidney problems. While you need protein to repair and build your muscles, an excessive amount can be harmful and fat producing. Coffee will give you an energy boost, but too much and you will experience jittery nerves, sleeplessness and stomach problems. You need vitamins and minerals, but take too many and you will be punished with everything from hair loss to stomach problems. You have to train hard in karate to progress, but if you go overboard, you risk health problems and injuries.

Never go by the creed that "more is better." Instead, consider this ancient Greek motto: "Nothing to excess, everything in moderation." One piece of chocolate cake is okay, but four pieces isn't (darn-it). Sixty minutes of sparring is optimum, but two hours is risky. A four-ounce streak is fine, but a 20-ounce steak clogs your heart and slows your muscles.

Moderation in everything.

PART TWO

MENTAL
TRAINING

5 ways

to Alleviate Stress

Times are stressful and stress is making us ill, causing injuries and ending lives prematurely. Modern living is no longer a casual walk in the park. Actually, we don't walk much at all, but rather run all day from stressful place to stressful place. Stress is hurting us in our jobs, in school, in our personal lives, and in our training. The good news is that there are ways to use karate to reduce stress, so that we can be healthy and continue to grow in all areas of our lives. While exercise in general is a great nerve calmer, simulated fighting and hard bag work is an especially effective way to relieve an overload of stress.

I believe the best way to alleviate stress is to make the effort yourself, that is, train alone. Training by your lonesome allows you to do exactly those things that you know mellows you. If it's hard bag work that does it, take 20 minutes and pummel away with your punches and kicks without being distracted by other students or being told to stop by your instructor. If working hand combinations in the mirror calms you, then do it as long as you want, because your instructor isn't there to tell you to move on to something else.

Will karate training completely eliminate stress from your life? Probably not, but it will make you calmer and better able to handle all those unpleasantries that come your way in any given day.

Here are ways to use your fighting art to help you survive another day in paradise. The nice side benefit is that not only will you be calmer and ultimately healthier, the training will make you a better fighter.

1. TRAIN HARD

When I had a particularly nasty day as a street cop, I never went drinking with the boys after work. Instead, I punched and kicked the stuffing out of my heavy bag or trained especially hard in my class that evening. Thirty minutes later, I was whistling a happy tune and ready to calmly take on the rest of the night. I did this without wasting money on booze and feeling like old roadkill the next morning from a hangover.

2. WORK OUT EARLY

If you are like me, kicking and punching a heavy bag is not the first thing you think about when you awaken to the morning sun sneaking through a crack in your curtains. Nonetheless, if you can draw on that world famous discipline of yours and drag yourself out of the rack and just do it, you will feel wonderful afterwards. Within minutes, your endorphins (a natural "drug" produced by your body when you train hard) are racing throughout your system, and by the time you hit the shower, you are mellow and better able to ward off the usual stressors that are about to come your way.

3. WORK YOUR BIG MUSCLES

The larger the muscle group you train, the more endorphins you release into your system. Doing three sets of 10 finger flicks at an imaginary set of eyes doesn't compare to the energy expenditure and the resultant outpouring of endorphins you get when you do three sets of 10 reps of sidekicks. Relative to the rest of your body, your legs, which include your butt, are your biggest muscles and require the greatest amount of energy to move.

If you have a stressful day coming up, or you have already had one, do two sets of 15 reps of all of your favorite kicks.

4. PUT ON SOME GOOD SOUNDS

Put on a CD of your favorite music and start kicking and punching. It doesn't matter what kind of music you like, as long as it connects mentally and spiritually with you (though I can't imagine alleviating stress listening to heavy metal, but admittedly I'm getting older).

5. TRAIN WITH A PARTNER

Okay, training with a partner isn't exactly solo training, but if you can find a person who wants what you want - a workout to alleviate stress - you still have some control over your training. And with a partner there are more things you can do than when training by yourself.

10 ways

to Use
Mental Imagery

It's frustrating when you can't get to your class because of illness, family obligations or some other thing that conflicts with your training schedule. Things are so crazy, you can't even get in a solo training session in your garage. Well, calm down, because all is not lost. There is another way to get in a practice session in - and you won't even get sweaty doing it. Hey, you don't even have to get out of bed.

I've written a great deal over the years about the importance of mental imagery - sometimes called visualization - and I believe in its power now more than ever. It has been of great value to me in my martial arts training and when I was a police officer dealing with thieves, rapists and killers, the kind of folks who get real cantankerous when you arrest them.

Volumes could be written about all that is involved mentally and physically with the mental imagery process, but I'm just going to give you a short teaser that I hope encourages you to research the subject further. My explanation is a simplistic one, though I think it's all you need to know at this point to understand why and how mental imagery can improve your fighting ability.

What Happens when you use Mental Imagery

This is a little dry, but read it anyway.

Studies show that while you are in a relaxed state of mind and visualizing your karate techniques, the neurons in your nervous system fire slightly as if your body were actually executing punches and kicks. Mental imagery strengthens neural patterns, which reinforce your neuro-muscular strengthening of neural patterns, which reinforce your neuro-muscular coordination. Get all that?

When you mentally rehearse karate techniques, you "educate" your subconscious mind, so that it later directs your body to reproduce what you rehearsed, whether you are in your karate school, tournament ring or a street self-defense situation. This works because your subconscious doesn't distinguish between reality and imagination. It thinks you physically practiced your kick/punch combination or kata. Later, when you go to do them for real, your body translates those mental images into your physical movements.

Use all your Senses

A common error when doing mental imagery is to only "see" the techniques in your mind's eye. Psychologists say that you should actually engage at least three of your five senses to enhance your visualization even more. For example, see your sidekick slice through the air. Hear your feet scoot on the floor as you lunge forward, and hear your pant leg snap in the air as your sidekick extends. Feel the muscles of your legs, hip, and butt drive it into the target.

Some sports champions say they use all five of their senses, finding that it triples the effectiveness of their mental imagery. So, in addition to the three senses we just used in the sidekick, include the taste of the sweat running down your face and the smell of the air in the gymnasium. While these aren't particularly pleasant images, the idea is to make your visualized world as vivid as you can.

Here are 10 ways to use mental imagery to help you fight better.

1. IMPROVING TECHNIQUE

First, get comfy in your easy chair, sofa, bed or on the floor. Close your eyes and induce deep relaxation, using whatever method you like. Once there, see yourself in your fighting stance, left leg forward and your hands in the on-guard position. See and feel your left backfist launch forward, followed a fraction of a second later by a lunge step with your left leg. See and feel your fist make contact with the heavy bag and hear the resounding smack. Feel the bag as you watch your hand sink into it. Feel your lunge step land a split second later. See and feel your backfist snap back.

When you visualize your backfist, see and feel it lash out at the same speed, with the same power and with the same mental intensity as you would use if you were really hitting the bag. Use as many of your senses as possible to make the image as real as you can. Your goal is to get so good at it that you perspire slightly and your pulse and breathing rate increases. Visualize 10 reps on each side.

Although you did the reps only in your mind while positioned comfortably in your favorite place to relax, your muscles think (deep in their little minds) that you really gave them a workout. When you get to your school the next day and throw those backfists for real against the bag, you will pop them out with a just a little more improvement than the last time you worked out in your school. This is because your mind and body believe that you got in an extra workout, which in a way, you did.

As an experiment, I once prepared for a big tournament using only visualization to practice my empty-hand kata, although I physically practiced my weapon's kata several times a week. I won fifth place with the weapons form, but I won my division and then overall grand champion with the one I practiced only in my mind.

2. EMOTIONAL PREPARATION

Every martial artist has workouts that are lousy and workouts that are great. Don't dwell on the lousy ones, but use your mental imagery to examine how you can reproduce those great ones.

Most likely your last workout was great because you were having fun and because everything went perfectly. Either the specifics of the workout itself were fun - the drills, exercises, laughter, a new technique, etc. - or maybe you just felt so good physically and emotionally that day that everything you did was flawless. You were so "up" that even an injury wouldn't have bothered you. It's this positive emotion that you want to reproduce every time you train. Here is how you do it using mental imagery.

Write Down how you Felt on a Good Day

Begin by writing down as many adjectives as you can that describes that great workout you had. For my last workout, for example, I would put down challenging, fun, smooth, fast, energetic, valuable, and powerful. Next, jot down a few thoughts you had during that great workout. Be sure to write them in the present tense. In my case I would put, "My movements are flowing easily tonight." "I am so good at this." "I am bursting with energy." "This is really practical," "Wow, I feel strong."

Lastly, write down how you think your body language was during that workout. When you feel lousy, you usually look lousy: you frown, your shoulders slump, and your back rounds like an old workhorse. But when you feel great, you stand taller, your shoulders are back and you got a big smile on your mug, or at least a feint one. But for this exercise, you are not concerned with that bad workout, but with the good one.

Sit in a comfortable place, get deeply relaxed and recall that training session when you were so hot and could do no wrong. Write down several descriptive words that apply to how you felt then. Recall your posture, facial expressions and your strong, positive walk. Lastly, remind yourself why you are training: fitness, fun, and self-defense.

By writing down all of these positive thoughts and images, you prepare yourself physically and mentally to perform at your best. To use computer speak: You *program* yourself. When you write, you have to first think about these things in a positive way. Positive thinking and positive writing - positive, positive, positive. All this adds up to creating a psychological response in your brain to bring out that positive emotional state you had during that last great workout.

By recalling all these positive elements, you connect with the emotion that creates a great workout and helps you progress.

Do this ritual regularly, and you will enjoy more great workouts than ever before. Do it in your car 15 minutes before class, in the bus that takes you to your workout, or in your home before your solo workout in the basement.

This works.

3. AFFIRMATIONS

This is closely linked to *#2, Emotional Preparation*, but different enough to warrant its own section. Although at first blush it might seem like some new-age mysticism straight out of California, it really does work, not only for your karate training, but in other areas of your life, too.

Affirmations are simply positive statements that you make to yourself mentally, out loud and in writing. They are a way of communicating to your subconscious mind, that portion of your brain that directs all your actions. Because you are loading only positive data into your subconscious, the directions it sends out can only be positive.

Let's say you have a belt exam in three weeks. How many times have you heard fellow students say things like "I will never be ready in time." "My kicks are so lousy." "I know I will screw up big time." Not surprisingly, they usually do poorly on their test because they programmed themselves to do poorly. As the computer geeks say: Garbage in, garbage out.

If this is you, stop doing that right now. Even if you are just trying to be humble around your friends, never, never, never use negative words about yourself. Always keep it positive. Use words like *Become, Get* and *Achieve*.

• I will BECOME a brown belt in three weeks

• I will GET promoted

• I will ACHIEVE my goal of earning my brown belt

Don't use words like *Want, Wish* and *Hope.* "I hope I pass." They are too weak, too unconvincing. Use words that already place you where you want to be.

Begin by writing each of these three positive statements down at least 15 times a day. Write them in the margin of your newspaper, on your lunch bag, on your notebook, on those little sticky notes and then stick them all over the place. Write fresh ones each day, so that your mind benefits from the exercise.

As you write these things down, say them aloud. "I will become a brown belt," and visualize your instructor awarding you the belt. See yourself tying it around your waist. Feel that elation from your accomplishment.

All three statements written 15 times makes for 45 positive statements. All three statements spoken aloud 15 times, makes for 45 verbal statements, which adds up to 90 affirmations. And remember, each time you write and say these things, you also see in your mind that belt being awarded to you. That is another 45 positive moments, which brings the grand total to 135 positive affirmations that direct you toward achieving that brown belt. Do this every day leading up to your test. It may sound like a lot of effort, but it takes no more than five to ten minutes, leaving you 23 hours and 50 minutes to do other things.

It's the best 10 minutes you can invest for yourself, because it will repay you 10 fold.

4. VISUALIZE YOUR HERO

Do you wish you could spar as well as Bruno, the senior brown belt in your class? He fights so courageously as he moves around his opponent with the grace of a cat, and then lunges forward with perfectly executed kicks and punches that land with loud thumps. You, however, move with the grace of a wino and your attacks rarely, if ever, get to the target. (Sigh) If only you could spar like Bruno . . .

You can, or at least come pretty close to it. Since you have watched him spar many times, you are able to form a vivid mental picture in your mind of his fighting style, everything from his opening salute to his way of stalking, blocking, punching and kicking. Up to now, you have always *looked at* him. Now you are going to see the world from his point of view.

Swapping Heads

Get comfy in your easy chair, close your eyes and take a few deep breaths. Feel your body weight sink more and more deeply into your chair each time you exhale. Take five or more minutes to get deeply relaxed (if you skip the relaxation step, the visualization that follows won't be as effective), and begin by seeing Bruno pull on his sparring gloves. But instead of looking *at* him, seeing him as you normally do, replace his head with yours so that you are now looking at the world from atop his shoulders (make sure your head is facing the right way). Look down and see yourself pull on that last glove, tighten whatever color belt he wears, shrug your shoulders to loosen them as he does, and then turn and face one of the students in class, preferably one you regularly spar with.

See and feel yourself salute your opponent and begin to move around him looking for openings. Here comes a front kick at you. Block it, just as Bruno would, and then lunge in, just like Bruno would do, and nail him with a strong reverse punch to his chest, just like Bruno always does. Scoot away, circle your opponent just like Bruno does and then explode forward with that beautiful backfist/sidekick combination he uses. Wow, both techniques got in, so you move back out of range and circle him again. Continue visualizing this match for several minutes, doing everything Bruno would do as you see the sparring match from atop his shoulders. Repeat this "head swapping" mental exercise once or twice a day for a couple weeks until you feel completely comfortable with the process.

The next step is to do it in class. Since you are unable to use the same relaxation exercises you do at home to induce deep relaxation, you have to do an abbreviated version. Instead of chatting with other classmates as you prepare to spar, use the minute or so it takes to get your gear on to allow for a few deep breaths to get relaxed and clear your mind. As you put on your gloves, once again imagine that you are Bruno and you are looking at everything from his shoulders. Salute your partner and begin sparring - as Bruno.

Of course head swapping with Bruno is not going to make you kick higher if you are not flexible or let you throw a perfect ridgehand strike if you have never learned to do so. But using visualization to fight as Bruno, helps you emulate his positive sparring attributes until they take on the characteristics of your personal fighting style.

5. VISUALIZE A HIGH-RISK MOMENT

Let's say your workday ends after the sun goes down, which means you always have to walk through the parking lot in the dark to get your car. There are a scattering of other cars and trucks on the lot, a dumpster in one corner, a four-foot high wall on one side at the far end, burnt-out street lights all around and, to top it off, the lot is in a high-crime neighborhood.

It's been my experience, having taught many personal safety classes, that most people are easily caught by surprise when they haven't given consideration to being victimized. Most people don't have a plan even when they have to function in a high-risk environment, such as our dark parking lot here. Then, when suddenly confronted with a threat, they are so fearful and amazed that they are about to be hurt or ripped off, they freeze in place and are unable to react.

A plan, especially a visualized plan, will help you act smoothly, almost as if you have been there and done that before. And in a way, you have, at least in your mind. Here is how you visualize a plan for that trek across the dangerous parking lot.

Know the Turf

Examine the lot in daylight and make note of all those danger spots I just pointed out, and then look at it again at night to note how darkness changes the look of things. Consider where your car is, what danger spots are closest to it and which ones you have to walk by. Now, imagine a mugger, a rapist, or a couple of skinheads stepping out from behind that dumpster and walking toward you. What if the threat came from behind that four-foot wall? How about if a half dozen street thugs step out of the shadows under the burnt-out street light? What if a man suddenly stands up from behind that car parked next to yours?

I have investigated dozens of situations exactly like these, and they continue to happen every day in this country, in every city in the nation.

Visualize your Response

Consider what you will do if you are suddenly confronted by any one of these threats. Will you run? Yell for help? Stand and fight? Pull a 9mm out of your pocket? Jump up and do a Jean-Claude Van Damme spinning kick? (Hopefully not the last one.)

By preplanning your response, you will act more smoothly when a real situation happens. While it may not occur exactly the way you visualized it, you will still react better than if you had never given it any thought at all. Preplan and stay alert to dangers while you are in a high-risk place and reduce the chance of your name appearing in the "Victim" column on a police report.

6. VISUALIZE A REAL CONFRONTATION

I use to patrol a district that had several rough and tumble taverns in which we were always getting calls on "unwanteds." As the name implies, an unwanted is a guy the bartender doesn't want in his place (inevitably, these guys are ex professional wrestlers).

I used mental imagery to rehearse making my approach on unwanteds, imagining what I would say, how I would grab a guy when he refused to leave on his own, how I would physically control him as we left the tavern, and how I would apply the handcuffs out on the sidewalk. I visualized this as I patrolled, when I parked at a busy street corner to watch passersby, and especially when I was driving to the scene of an unwanted call.

Did any of my calls go down exactly as I had visualized? No. But they happened similarly enough that my mental rehearsal made my actions smoother than if I would have responded to the call completely cold.

Usually, the salivating, over-drunk guy was at the end of the bar or sprawled in a booth in the back corner of the place. I was able to approach him with confidence because I had already approached him many times - in my mind. I was able to talk calmly and with confidence as I ordered him to leave, because I had practiced the words before. When he told me to go and stuff it, I was able to reach for him with confidence and skill because I had already done it so many times in my mind. I was able to walk him out of the joint and slap on the handcuffs as smoothly as can be because, you guessed it, I had rehearsed the actions many times in my mind.

Here are a few common high-risk scenarios that you can apply mental imagery to so that your actions are smooth and rehearsed.

- School bully
- Work bully

- Angry motorist
- Drunken brother-in-law

- A street thug
- A mentally deranged person

Make yourself
familiar with your
parking lot.

What would
you do in this
situation?

You know who the adversaries are in your life. If there is any chance your contact with them could turn violent, it would behoove you to prepare with mental imagery. Visualize how it might happen and visualize your attempts to stop it from escalating. But just in case that doesn't work, visualize your physical response.

While the real situation may not happen exactly as you saw it in your mind, by thinking about and visualizing your actions, your response will be smoother than if the situation was to catch you completely unprepared.

7. VISUALIZE WINNING

For several days before your next tournament competition, spend time visualizing your win. Tell yourself that you are a winner and that the big, gaudy trophy is yours. Tell yourself that you will compete like a champion because you *are* a champion.

See yourself at the conclusion of the event standing strong and with confidence from having just performed at your very best. See yourself being handed that trophy. See yourself reach out and grasp it in your hands. Feel its weight. Feel how good it is in your hands. See yourself raise it above your head and smile as you show it to your friends and family in the crowd. Hear them cheer and whistle. Feel the energy you have at that moment and how good it makes you feel.

Back in the 1960s and 1970s, Chuck Norris used mental imagery every time he competed. Today, virtually every competitor in the Olympics uses mental imagery to see themselves on the victory stand.

8. VISUALIZE YOUR GOAL

A powerful resolution to be the best one can be is one of the many differences that separates a champion martial artist (you can define champion how ever you want) from the person who is just going through the motions. Some people use the word "heart" to describe such a person. "She has heart," they say, meaning that she puts all that she has into her training to reach her goal.

People who don't have a clear goal are the ones who ask themselves "Why am I doing this? Why am I putting myself through this pain and strain? Why should I do all this when I can just buy a gun to protect myself?" They ask these questions because they don't have a clear, solid plan for what they want out of their karate training.

On the other hand, people who have a clear goal in their minds never ask themselves why they are training so hard because they know why. They are training for their next belt exam. They are training hard so they can compete at their best in the next tournament. They are training hard to have more confidence to face life's challenges and dangers.

When you know where you are going and how you are going to get there - you will never ask yourself why you are doing it.

9. VISUALIZE A GOOD CLASS

Tonight is your sparring class and you dread it. You are convinced you are rotten at it, you know you will jam your already-sore toe on someone's shin, and there is no doubt in your mind that every sparring partner is going to beat you to a pulp.

When you consider everything you have read up to this point on mental imagery, can you see how negative and destructive this kind of thinking is? You can't force yourself to like every aspect of your karate training, but you can mentally condition yourself to grow from every part of it, even those things you don't like to do. I've seen students use affirmations and visualization to actually turn themselves around and start to enjoy a part of karate they had always disliked.

Usually, though not always, you hate something because you are not good at it. Can you think of anything you excel at, but hate doing? Probably not. Whether you like or don't like a particular phase of karate is not important. What is, is that you program yourself to grow from the experience.

Seeing a Great Class

Schedule yourself to get to your class 15 minutes early. Stay in your car and get as comfortable and as relaxed as you can. Now, begin your internal chat.

We are sparring in class tonight. The butterflies I feel in my stomach are bubbles of energy flitting about and wanting to escape through my fast and powerful punches and kicks. I am brave and I am courageous. No matter who I spar tonight, I will do my best and learn from the experience. Some of my techniques will get blocked and some of my opponent's attacks will get by my defense. When that happens, I will be brave and continue sparring. I will learn from the error. After all, that is why I am here: to learn. If I get hit extra hard, I will continue sparring. I will understand that I got hit because my block missed or I didn't see the blow coming at all. I will learn from that. I am getting better at sparring. It is fun. I am learning more and more about my techniques and how best to apply them. I am improving with each partner and with each sparring class.

Feel free to change this self-talk to fit your particular needs. Keep all your statements positive and use lots of powerful adjectives. Have this chat with yourself when you first awaken in the morning, again on your lunch break and once more just before class.

You may never love sparring, but this exercise will help you grow each time you do it.

10. VISUALIZE BEING BETTER LOOKING

This worked amazingly well for me.

I'm kidding, of course. My point is that although mental imagery is an extraordinary mental force, you nonetheless have to stay within attainable objectives. If you were born missing a left arm, you are wasting your time visualizing a fast left punch. If you have naturally short legs, visualization isn't going make them grow longer. You have to work within the boundaries of what nature gave you, or didn't.

On the other hand, don't short change yourself, either. If your left arm is missing, you can use mental imagery to help you become the best right-armed fighter you are capable of. Even though you were born with the legs of a dachshund, you can use the power of mental imagery to help you turn those short legs into an asset. If you were born with a particular *something* (don't ever think or say the word "handicap" or "limitation"), you need to analyze it to be absolutely sure that it's really something that will never improve. Qualities like extremes in height, an abnormal arm or leg, a blind eye, and extreme curvature of the spine, are all permanent and visualizing them away isn't going to work. Nonetheless, you can still use mental imagery to work around them to bring out your best in those things you can do.

Never look at anything as a limitation. Figure out what are your capabilities and strong points and use visualization to make them even better.

Even the Old Street Fighters Visualize

As I have researched mental imagery over the years, I have not been surprised to see it being used by the new generation of martial artists, especially since there has been such a proliferation of information about its effectiveness. What has been surprising, however, was to discover that so many of the old veteran street fighters I have met also use it. I'm talking about guys who have arrived at their place in the martial arts world not by playing "tag karate" in tournaments, but by thrashing around on the streets and in tough bars with some mean hombres.

I call these guys "meat and potato" fighters because they have no interest in fancy and frilly techniques. They rely on solid basics that aren't pretty but nonetheless get the job done. One would think that these guys would laugh off mental imagery training as being "new age nonsense." But not so. These meat and potato veteran fighters use it for one reason.

It works.

10 ways

to Eat Pain

"Eat pain?" you ask. "I don't want to eat pain. I don't want to feel pain at all."

Well, then you are participating in the wrong activity; you might want to consider stamp collecting since there is no way you can avoid getting owies when you train in the martial arts.

When I began training in the mid 1960's, we didn't have any of the protective equipment we enjoy today. Those first three years of training were painful, as I always had a body part bandaged and at least two walnut-sized swellings on the back of my hands, shins and the tops of my feet. And we always had blood splatters on our uniforms. Red Badges of Courage we called the stains, and we took great pride in them. To get some relief from the slams and bams against already swollen parts, I would go to a mattress store to buy large squares of foam rubber, cut them into smaller pieces and tape them over my injured parts.

Happily, those times are gone because protective equipment is plentiful now. Nonetheless, pain is still part of karate training. Blows aren't always pulled and accidents happen. Of course, there is full-contact fighting where pain is deliberate as well as street fights where pain is intentional. So how do you deal with it? How do you keep going when pain is ripping through your body? How do you face another match when you know there will be pain involved?

Here are five ways to eat the pain.

1. GET USED TO IT

Can you really get used to pain? Well, sort of. You will never get to a point where pain doesn't hurt, but you can reach a stage where getting hit just isn't that big a deal.

Most beginners start out being afraid, so they flinch and overreact to even the slightest smack with a padded glove or shoe. But a month later, these same people are getting hit a little harder and reacting less. By the time they have earned a couple of belts, they have progressed to a point where they barely notice getting clobbered. They have arrived; they are on the road to getting conditioned to eat pain.

In the Street

There are some styles that don't allow contact at all in their training. This is a serious mistake. Whenever I have seen students who have trained in such schools, they inevitably pull their kicks and punches far too short, sometimes as much as twelve inches from the target. Remember: *How you train is how you will fight for real.* Training this way will come back to haunt you in a real fight when you unhappily discover your blows falling short.

Secondly, training to miss doesn't help your training partner to get conditioned to take a hit, even a light one. When I have gotten these transfer students, some with as much as two years of training under their belts, I've seen them overreact to even a light tap. If they were in a real fight and reacted this way to a blow, their disrupted focus would make them vulnerable to getting hit even more.

In Competition

I've also seen tournament fighters lose a match because they overreacted to an uncontrolled blow. While excessive contact usually gets a fighter disqualified or at least a warning, it's not going to get called as such when the judges don't see it. What often happens is that the unconditioned fighter reacts to getting hit, stops fighting and, to his chagrin, his opponent takes advantage of the moment and hits him again. The judges see the second blow and award it a point.

If you get hit hard in a tournament, keep fighting. If the judges saw it, they will stop the match. If they didn't see it, you want to maintain your focus and continue to be on guard against anything your opponent does.

Here is a favorite drill of mine that will quickly condition you to take a hit.

Three-person Drill

I learned this many years ago from kenpo Professor Rick Alamany. It can be used for many purposes, such as a blocking drill, a reaction drill and a way to work combinations. But for our purposes here, let's use it as a way to get conditioned to getting hit.

Assume your fighting stance between two training partners and face one of them. He will throw a roundhouse kick at your front thigh and hit it with medium impact. The moment his kick lands, you respond with a backfist to his head. You then turn and face your other training partner and allow him to kick you in the front thigh with a medium-impact, roundhouse kick. Again you respond with a backfist.

That's the drill. You turn left and get hit, and you turn right and get hit. Fun, huh? Continue doing this for a set of 10-15 blows from each partner. This is good for you in two ways. First, you get conditioned to take a hit. You feel it, you hear it and you tolerate it. Secondly, you condition yourself to instantly hit back every time you get struck. Instead of reflexively saying "ouch," you reflexively return a blow of your own.

When you get used to this, and it may take anywhere from one workout session to 10, your training partners raise their kicks to your midsection. Respond to their solid hits to your belly with a backfist to their head. In the third stage, your partners hit you with medium impact to your forehead (make sure they are wearing their padded gloves), and you respond with a counter, say a reverse punch to their middle.

You should make only light contact against your outside partners. The drill is to teach you to react with a counterattack when you get hit. If you were to hit your outside partners as solidly as they hit you, they should technically respond with a counter of their own. That would complicate the drill too much, if it didn't turn into a brawl first. To prevent this, respond with a controlled tap.

As you can see, you can get quite creative with this using different offensive and countering techniques. The beauty of it is that you quickly condition yourself to getting hit. Before you know it, getting whacked extra hard in class will no longer be a big deal.

Let's look at pain from the standpoint of the physical, emotional, mental, and spiritual.

Three-Person Drill

The outside training partner connects with a hard roundhouse kick to your thigh . . .

. . . to which you respond with a backfist.

The other outside person connects with a hard round-house kick ...

... and again you respond immediately with a back-fist. When you get used to taking a hard kick to the legs, your training partners should raise their kicks to your abdomen.

2. PHYSICAL

Besides being mentally conditioned to taking a hit, it's important that you are in good physical condition, too. The term "hardbody" was never more apropos than when referring to your physical ability to absorb a punch or kick. A strong body, one that is padded with muscle, will better absorb a blow than a frail one. By the way, I've struck some overly fat guys with my police baton only to have them look at me as if I were wasting my time and theirs, which in a way I was. Fat is padding, too, but I'm in no way advocating that you overdose on burgers and fries so you can take a punch.

It's also good to have a strong neck. The less your head moves when struck, the less your brain gets jarred and the more awake you stay so you can keep on slugging it out.

Adrenaline is probably nature's best buffer to pain. I once saw a guy get his ear cut completely off in a knife assault, and he was so busy fighting that he didn't notice it until my police partner and I pointed out that it was lying under a parked car. A flood of adrenaline blocks pain when you are high on rage and fear. Once the fight is over, however, the aches and pains begin.

3. EMOTIONAL

Out-of-control rage is an emotion that can easily cause you to forget all of your training. When your friend tells you that he got so mad in a fight that he had to be pulled off the guy, he is also telling you that he was out of control. That is not a good thing. Fighting is about control of yourself, the other person and the situation. It's impossible to control anything if you are so out of it that you have to be physically restrained.

Anger is not necessarily a bad thing as long as it's directed and used to your advantage. If someone attacks you or a loved one, you should be outraged by that - but the rage should be controlled and channeled to facilitate your warrior spirit and buffer your pain.

Pride and the fear of embarrassment are powerful emotions that help you tolerate getting hit. There you are fighting in a tournament as all of your classmates cheer you on. Wham! You take a hard shot in the gut. Is that your morning cornflakes rising to the surface? Your classmates don't know how hard you got hit, and you don't want to show them that you can't take a punch to the ol' breadbasket, so you fight on because your fear of losing face in front of them is more powerful than the blow. You ate the pain.

I was in a tournament once fighting an opponent who was not only a good karate man but a Golden Gloves boxer. At one point, he punched me so hard in the ribs that I saw visions of my ancestors coming over on the Mayflower. I wanted to drop into a ball on the floor and roll around, but all my buddies were cheering me on, unaware of the severity of the blow. I plodded on somehow, long enough to finish the round, and lose the match. I was able to finish because I drew on my pride to stay in there and fight.

I saved face, though I had a bruise the shape of a fist on my ribs that took two weeks to fade and two months for the tenderness to go away.

4. PSYCHOLOGICAL

Your mental focus is important to your ability to withstand pain in a fight. If you go into a competition, street fight or a hard sparring session in your school with confidence in your ability, your mental focus will enable you to eat more pain. You will view a hard kick in the stomach or a whack in the face as just the cost of doing business on your way to defeating your opponent.

On the flip side, if you are not confident in your ability, or you are convinced your opponent is going to beat you into the dirt, he probably will, and he will inflict a lot of pain in the process. If you have a mind-set that you are going to lose, not only will your conviction be fulfilled, you will feel every blow that it takes to accomplish it.

Instead, go into the battle convinced that you will win and that any pain you receive is just an annoyance on your way to victory.

5. SPIRITUAL

Let's define spirit here as your will to keep on fighting. If all the other elements discussed in this section are not strong or present, your will to fight after you have been hurt will dissipate quickly.

I've known people with a tremendous will who have never had a karate lesson or any other kind of self-defense training. When the situation called for it, however, they were more than willing to get in there and fight. They had a warrior spirit that came to them naturally, a spirit that kept them fighting no matter how much pain they received. They had little skill, but their will was mighty, and they stayed in the fight all the way to the conclusion.

If you are not born with this kind of spirit, you must train hard to develop it. The harder you practice, the greater the confidence you will have that you are a winner. Train so that you believe in yourself and in your warrior spirit. When you achieve this, you will have the will to continue fighting no matter how much pain you have to eat.

10 ways

to Learn Quickly

Besides wanting to know how to improve speed, power and strategy, the other typical question in the minds' of karate students is how they can more quickly achieve the ability to apply new techniques reflexively and with perfection under the stress of competition or self-defense.

Ingrain

This is a word I use often when I'm teaching. I want my students to have the technique, principle or concept ingrained into their brain and muscles. In five minutes I can teach them an effective way to get their foot into their opponent's abdomen, and at the end of those few minutes, they will be able to demonstrate the technique and mimic all the elements of the movement. But will they be able to do it on the street when they are suddenly forced to defend themselves against a big, nasty attacker who wants to do them serious harm? I would never bet on them.

Hey, a parrot can mimic, but it can't carry on a conversation. After five minutes of working on a new technique, you are only mimicking the movement. Not enough effort and not enough time has yet been invested to get it deeply ingrained into your mind so that it becomes an automatic response. Many students lose sight that their objective in learning the fighting arts is to make their knowledge instinctual. Fighting is too fast and furious to have to think about the mechanics of a particular movement.

The good news is that it's not that difficult to get a technique ingrained into your muscles and brain, but it does require effort. Here are five ways to do it.

1. REPS

Ah yes, reps. You have heard that here before, right? Well, here it is again, because as I've said, if there is a secret to success in the martial arts, it's repetitions - lots and lots of repetitions. In fact, one Japanese master said that you truly don't know a technique until you have performed it 100,000 times. While I think you can ingrain a technique sooner than that, if you were to do a technique 100,000 times, the movement would be as automatic as your breathing.

Some students are information junkies: They want to learn something new every class. Unfortunately, such an approach doesn't lead to skill since the material learned last session has yet to be ingrained. Be wary of instructors who bombard you with new material in a poor attempt to keep you motivated. A good instructor should be able to keep you interested and enthused by giving you a variety of drills to work the so-called old material.

Casey Eberting is a teaching professional in the sport of golf. I have no idea if he has ever thrown a roundhouse kick, but he teaches the same thing I do about the value of repetitions. This is what he says.

"What I have observed, and what the studies mention, is that it takes a certain amount of time for the body to learn a simple motion, much longer than most of you would imagine. I, therefore, recommend for my students to practice a new motion for at least three to four weeks (if practicing regularly) before moving on to something new. If you do any less, you run the risk of not learning the motion, or you may only partially learn it, depending on how often and over how long of a time span you practice."

For definition purposes, learning occurs when a conscious effort to put the body in a particular position or to move it in a certain way is transformed from a conscious action to an automatic action, requiring no thought.

I discuss many ways to do repetitions throughout this book. I can't encourage you enough to use them and make up more ways on your own. The only rule in rep practice is that you do them correctly, you do them routinely - at least once a week - and you do them with complete concentration. Shoot for 200 reps a week with a new technique.

2. MENTAL IMAGERY

Refer to *10 Ways to Use Mental Imagery* (page 241). I believe that visualizing a technique, when done properly, is so powerful that you can count it as part of your reps for the week. If you do 200 reps on a new combination during your classes and do 50 visualized reps of the same technique on the weekend, you can claim 250 reps for the week. Visualization is that effective.

3. VERBALIZE THE TECHNIQUE TO SOMEONE

This is a method I learned when I was attending an FBI firearms instructor school. It's an excellent way to ingrain a new technique because you are forced to analyze all the mechanics of the movement, sort them out in your brain and then verbalize them so that your explanation is understandable to a listener.

Say you learn a new move tonight in class, a lead-arm uppercut. On your way home, verbalize the mechanics of the technique as if you were talking to a person who knows nothing about karate. If you are in the privacy of your own car, give your explanation out loud. If you are on a bus or just walking along the sidewalk, it's probably best to *think* them to yourself to prevent people from staring.

Anyway, begin your explanation to your invisible student (or that invisible friend you always talk with) as to how he should position his feet, angle his upper body and how his arms are to be held prior to delivering the blow. Next, articulate what his feet and upper body are to do in conjunction with his thrusting uppercut. Explain how his hips snap, his shoulder rotates, the angle his fist travels, what happens to his other arm, where to look, what his muscles do upon impact, and what his attacking arm, upper body and feet do after he has struck the target.

Teach a Friend

Another way to verbalize a new technique, or even an old one, is to teach a training partner. In the FBI shooting school, we would pair up with another student after learning a new shooting position, and talk him through the position as if he had never heard of it before. It forced us to think hard about all the elements in the technique because the student was instructed to do exactly what he was told. If we used a slang expression, he would act as if he didn't understand. If we said something like "point at the target" and we had yet to tell him to remove his gun from its holster, he would simply point at it with his finger.

It's been my experience that when a person can clearly verbalize a technique, he has a greater understanding of the movement.

4. VERBALIZE TO YOURSELF

You can do this exercise in your school, but be warned that you might get a reputation as being a weirdo. I think it's best to do it when you are alone, like in the bathroom. The exercise is for you to talk to yourself, or more specifically, talk to your subconscious brain in order to better ingrain in your gray matter the specific technique you want there.

Consider a block/backfist/reverse punch combination. When you execute this movement, your eyes see what is going on and communicate with your brain about it. When you add to this process, that is, you talk aloud as you do the movement, you trigger those parts of your subconscious that hear, speak and see, which affects your memory and learning. Studies show that when students vocalize what they are doing, they have a 90-percent retention rate.

Your subconscious brain will instinctively learn to listen to what you have to say, especially if you say it with conviction and with words that are positive. When it has absorbed your input, it then directs your conscious brain to do the right thing. Here is an example of what you can say using the block/backfist/reverse punch combination.

- I am brave and courageous as the assailant approaches.
- I am in control of myself.
- I am powerful and full of energy.
- The assailant throws a punch at my midsection.
- I whip my left arm down and easily block his punch.
- My right hand snaps into a high guard next to the right side of my face.
- My left hand snaps a backfist against the side of his face.
- As my backfist snaps back, I immediately launch my powerful reverse punch.
- My hips rotate forcefully forward.
- My explosive punch sinks deeply into his solar plexis.

Notice that the choice of words are descriptive and cover the basic elements of the combination. The sentences are short, making them easily absorbed by the subconscious brain. Don't use negatives, such as "I *won't* forget to rotate my hips," because when using words like "won't," your subconscious doesn't "hear" the negative word. It only hears "I forget to rotate my hips." Keep all of your statements positive, and use lots of descriptive adjectives and adverbs.

Your subconscious loves words like powerful, fast, snap, quick and explosive. Use lots of them.

Notice that the first three statements instill you with courage and self-control. This ingrains into your mind that you will face a situation with a warrior spirit. Also notice that you didn't use negatives, such as "I am not afraid." Keep everything positive.

Practice your combination 10 times and talk yourself through it each of those times. Use this learning method when practicing single techniques, combinations, sparring drills, kata practice and any other aspect of your training.

5. TRAINING WITH A PARTNER

Although you can learn a new technique from a video or magazine, you have to train with a live partner to experience that all-important *feel* that only a human can give you, such as the intricacies of distancing, timing, sudden range changes, how to deal with his speed and power, how it feels being blocked, and many other important elements.

Use your training partner wisely. Nothing annoys me more than seeing two partners in class gabbing about a technique rather than practicing it. If you want to talk about it, do it later. But when you have that live body in front of you, take advantage of the time and get as many educational reps in as you can.

6. UNSTRUCTURED PRACTICE

Use unstructured practice after you have worked hard on the first four phases. Unstructured practice consists of free sparring and drills that are not prearranged. When you have trained sufficiently in the first four phases, the technique will be ingrained into your subconscious mind so that it explodes out of you during your unstructured practice with little or no thought. When that happens, you have arrived.

You have learned.

7. SHORTER TRAINING SESSIONS

Recent studies show that shorter but more frequent training yields better results. This isn't one of those stupid info commercials that claim you will develop incredible abdominal muscles in three minutes a day. What I'm advocating is that you have one to three 20-minute workouts a week outside of your regular class and cram as much practice as you can into the sessions.

One of my favorite ways to work out on the weekends is to do a 20-minute training session with my wife or daughter. We do a warmup, including a few dozen abdominal crunches, and then we train on whatever we want to emphasize that day. We don't waste a second of time, in fact we use the 20 minutes as a aerobic session, too.

A Poor Example

I once attended an eight-hour and brutally exhausting police training class that qualified attendees to teach a new police baton. When it was over and everyone was gathering their bags and preparing to leave, I heard several officers saying, "What a workout! That's was the best training I've ever had."

With all due respect to those guys, who were not martial artists, they didn't know what they were talking about. They were simply judging the class by how sweaty and fatigued they were. It was sweat producing, but it was also the worse training I had ever been involved in. The long session overtrained everyone, there were too many injuries, and the last hour undid everything the first seven hours tried to do.

While the class had many problems, the biggest one was its length. An eight-hour intensive training session is not conducive to good learning. If the training would have been broken in to four, two-hour sessions or, better yet, eight, one-hour sessions spread over eight days, the officers would have been far better trained

Do a Test

Choose a technique that you are having trouble with, say, a combination in which you lunge forward, kick, punch, step again, punch, punch and kick. Choose two or three non-class days, and work hard for 20 minutes on this complex combination. Don't go over 20 minutes no matter how good you feel once you get going. Cram that session with as many reps as you can squeeze in. Do them slowly, at medium speed and, when you are ready, at fast speed. Do this for two weeks and then note your progress.

You will be impressed.

8. LISTEN TO THE SLOW LEARNERS

I know a competitive bodybuilder who has won a ton of trophics and deservedly so because he has an incredible physique. I use to workout with him and watch with amazement as he would sit on the end of a bench and simultaneously chat with a friend, munch a cupcake, drink a soda pop and pump out 30 reps of biceps curls with a 20-pound dumbbell. He broke every rule in the book and yet his arms were awesome.

So is this the way all of us should lift weights? Of course not. He gets away with it because he is blessed with superior genetics, so much so that he could do everything wrong, which he did, and still look awesome. There are martial artists like this, too. Legendary Bill "Superfoot" Wallace has incredible kicking skills and has won many full-contact fights. Yet he freely admits that he fuels his body with junk food, in particular, hamburgers. I know another champion who never stretches and never warms up before he trains or competes, yet he can kick like a mule, and he almost always wins.

Should we emulate these people? Again, an emphatic, no. These people are naturals (maybe the term should be "unnaturals"). All we can do is look at them with envy and mumble nasty things about them under our breath.

We mortals must emulate those experts who have had to sweat and strain every step of the way. They had to painstakingly figure out which drills, supplemental exercises, diets, and workout schedules worked best for their average genetics and, in some cases, below average genetics. These are the guys we want to learn from.

Don't Follow Blindly

Let me emphasize this once more: Just because a champion trains or eats in a particular way, does not make it right. I've seen a lot of big names train completely wrong, yet still they were champions. But I've also seen them suffer with injuries as they got older when all those improper ways caught up with them.

If you have doubts about a training regimen, spend time researching it. Consider contacting the International Sport Sciences Association, ISSA. This is a body that certifies fitness instructors; they even have a specialist in martial arts conditioning. Consider contacting a sports medicine specialist in your area and researching the library and Internet for information. While this might take a little time, it will save you years of training incorrectly, years that as you age will come back to "bite" you in the form of nagging injuries.

Look Hard at a New Program

When you see a routine that a big name star is using and it looks like a good one to you, ask yourself the following questions before you take it on.

• Does the program conflict with existing information in sports medicine?
• Is the program appropriate for what you want out of the fighting arts?
• Is it progressive, meaning does it increase in increments as opposed to doing an all-out training marathon?

If you can answer these questions in the affirmative, then give it a try. But if you answer any with a negative, forget it and keep on searching.

I made a lot of mistakes coming up through the ranks and, because I'm such a nice guy, I'm trying to save you some aches and pains.

(I'll be right back. I gotta go get a couple aspirin.)

9. DON'T DO THE SAME THING EVERYDAY

Remember this simple rule: You can't make progress when you do the same thing every day.

I know people who run every day. I've also had karate people tell me that they drill on their backfist every day, or work the heavy bag every day. Not surprisingly, these are the same people who have frequent injuries and illnesses. The reason: overtraining.

Keep this absolute in the forefront of your mind and on the front page of your training journal. *You grow when you rest.* That's it, plain and simple. When someone says they are improving their reverse punch by doing 1,000 reps a day, they are fooling themselves and inviting regression and injury.

As I write this, my legs are a little shaky from a hard leg workout last night. Besides the usual drills and rep session, we finished the class with five sets of 10 reps of an exercise we call "sticky foot." As you may recall when I described it earlier, it involves kicking out slowly, holding out your leg in the locked position for one second, followed by raising it stiff-legged another three or four inches. It's a killer. We did one set for the back kick, one set for the chambered portion of the roundhouse, two sets for the front kick and one set for the sidekick.

My plan this morning was to do some kicking drills. Forget about it. My legs are too shaky, which is a clear indicator they need more rest. Instead, I'll do some hand drills, or bobbing and weaving drills. The legs get the day off.

Rotate the exercises in your training for optimal results.

10. HAVE A TRAINING OBJECTIVE

Sports psychologists have found that by developing a plan of attack for your training, you enhance your concentration as well as your ability to learn. This is especially easy to do when you are training by yourself or with a partner outside of your regular class, because you have more control over the direction of the training.

When Solo Training

If your workout is a solo one, it's important that you know in your mind what you want to get out of the session. "I want to work on polishing my sidekick" or "I want to work on faster gap closing techniques." It's okay to have a general goal, such as "I want to burn off that birthday cake I had yesterday." But you also need to have one that is a little more specific, such as, "As I burn off all of yesterday's cake, I will improve my lunging backfist."

Partner Training

If you are going to work out with a partner, you should both agree as to what you want out of the session. If you want to work hands, but he wants to work kicks - that isn't a problem. All you have to do is devise drills that involve both. The bottom line is that the two of you have an objective going into the training, and that you finish satisfied you got out of it what you wanted.

Class Training

When you are commuting to class, think about what you want to gain out of the instruction. Although you don't have control over the training as you do when working out by yourself and with one partner, you can still have an objective. "I'm going to make all of my kicks quick and with fast retractions," or "When we spar tonight, I'm going to throw lots of accurate combinations." You have to keep your objective general since you probably don't know what your teacher has in mind for the class. But you do know there will be punches and kicks, so design your plan around that.

Only with a real live partner can you experience the feel of a technique.

Stay Motivated

By having a clear objective for each training session, whether it's solo, with a partner or in your regular class, you go into it more motivated and stay motivated for the entire session. Studies show that top athletes always go into their training with a positive outlook, even when their training is going poorly. If their kicks feel sluggish or their accuracy is so poor during a workout that they couldn't hit a barn with their reverse punch, they don't allow that to make them angry or depressed. Instead, they analyze what is going on and figure out how to not let it happen again.

Surviving the Dumps

Reaching your big training goal is a step-by-step process in which there are many challenges and obstacles. One of the biggest obstacles are those occasional periods of low motivation. There is nothing terribly wrong when you have these moments; in fact, they are to be expected. Everyone has them, though not everyone survives them. Those who do survive are those people who have specific objectives for each training session. They understand that without objectives they have no direction and they are just treading water.

If you still feel your motivation is poor even when you have a clear training objective in your mind, you might consider taking a couple weeks off, even a month. This will give you a chance to analyze your approach and identify exactly what you need to be doing to reach your next goal. You might find, and this is more common than you think, that you are overtraining and getting burned out. Cutting back on your training will replenish your energy stores, which in turn will recharge your motivation.

5 ways

to Conquer Fear

Hearing all the stories of the great battles of the samurai would lead you to believe that they were warriors of great courage. Yes, they were brave, but they weren't fearless. While many of them consumed large quantities of sake prior to a fight (today we call this wine-bottle courage), others developed a philosophy of life that helped them to face the deadly blades of their enemies.

According to martial artist/Japanese historian/author Dave Lowry, who writes a column for *Black Belt* magazine called "The Karate Way," children of the samurai class were expected to conduct themselves with a dignity that emphasized their courage. To test their bravery, boys as young as seven were made to deliver messages to distant relatives, which required them to travel alone through deep forests, dangerous lands, frightening cities and even cemeteries they were told were haunted. As they grew into teenagers, they were made to witness executions. By the time these children had grown into young samurai they were calloused to violent confrontations (not unlike today's gang members).

This is not to say they weren't concerned about dying on the battle fields. Actually, they thought about it so much that they wrote volumes on the subject that are still studied today. For example, an early 18th century samurai named Tsunetomo Yamamoto wrote a treatise on dying called *Hagakure* (*Hidden Among the Leaves*) In it, he said, "The realization of certain death should be renewed every morning. Each morning you must prepare yourself for every kind of death. With composure of mind, imagine yourself broken by bows, guns, spears, swords, carried off by floods, leaping into a huge fire, struck by lightening, torn by earthquake, plunging from a cliff, and as a disease-ridden corpse."

Gee, what a fun guy.

Yamamoto and other samurai knew that fear couldn't be eliminated, but that it could be controlled and used to their benefit. By thinking about fear every day, especially the fear of death, they could neutralize it and divert it into energy to help them fight.

Today, fear still exists in our lives, at least in the lives of sane people who understand that the world is a scary place. As a martial artist and a person living in an increasingly dangerous world, you must accept the fact that you cannot completely escape fear. Nor should you. You can, however, take steps to control it and use it to your advantage.

Here are five ways.

1. UNDERSTAND THE SYMPTOMS

You are suddenly face to face with a huge, ugly guy you just know has his picture in the dictionary next to two words: *ugly* and *head-ripper-offer.* You have such a case of the pre-fight shakes that you could mix a protein drink just by holding it. Your mouth is a desert with dead sage brush, your teeth are making chipmunk noises, your arms and legs are as weak as your grandmother's, and you have a serious need to hit the potty. This is what fear feels like.

No matter how good you become in the fighting arts, you will always experience some or all of these feelings. Accept them as a natural part of your body's reactions, but don't let them create negative thoughts in your mind, such as "Oh man, he's going to kill me." Don't allow superficial elements to psyche you, like his skull tattoos, black clothing and killer gaze; you know those things can't hurt you. Draw upon your mental imagery, your positive affirmations and all those countless hours of physical training to overcome all negative and destructive thoughts.

Have confidence and faith in your training and ability.

2. TURN BUTTERFLIES INTO ENERGY

Every time I drove to a karate tournament to compete, those two-dozen zany butterflies in my stomach fluttered their wings harder and harder the closer I got. Once I was there and my time to compete drew closer, the winged creatures were having an all-out riot inside of me. But I never thought of the sensation as a negative one. I told myself that each of those butterflies was stirring up incredible energy in my body, and the only way I was going to release it was through my fast and powerful techniques.

When I was preparing to raid a dope house as a police officer or I was getting ready to take down an armed robber, I again used those butterflies to give me courageous energy that I released through my well-trained police techniques.

Butterflies are your Friends

Today, when I give a belt promotion examination in my martial arts school, I tell the candidates, as they stand nervously at attention before the test begins, to think of all those butterflies dancing madly in their stomachs as a source of energy. I tell them not to think of the fluttery sensation as uncomfortable, but rather a dynamic source of energy that will make them strong, fast and courageous.

3. DEVELOP YOUR FIGHTING SKILL

Nothing reduces fear like knowing you possess highly-developed skill in your chosen fighting art. When you progressively train to be your physical best, you won't completely eliminate fear (only fools are fearless), but you will develop greater confidence to face fearful situations.

Allow me to exaggerate to make a point. If you learn a new kata on Monday and then enter a tournament next Saturday, your level of fear is going to be much greater than if you entered a tournament after practicing your kata hundreds of times over a two-year period. Likewise, if you have been practicing only on flashy, "tag" techniques for tournament sparring, but one day you are confronted on the street by a nasty and tattooed, 225-pound ex-convict, the possibility that you will soil your trousers is pretty darn good.

Learn Systematically

First, build a solid foundation of basic techniques - backfist, reverse punch, jab, front kick, roundhouse kick - before you learn flashier ones. While my approach to the fighting arts is slanted toward street self-defense, I still think it's okay to have fun in the arts and learn some flashy techniques. But, and this is a big but, you must first build a solid foundation of basics, because without the foundation, you will have a hard time doing the fancy moves. In addition, it's those foundation techniques you will fall back on in a real situation. I was in dozens of street brawls as a police officer, and not once did I do a leaping, spinning kick like Jean-Claude Van Damme (like I ever could, anyway).

4. STAY IN SHAPE

There isn't anything that feels quite as good as when you are in top physical condition. Your muscles are taught and shapely and your cardiovascular system can handle long arduous workouts or an explosive all-out fight. Your confidence soars and those things that used to intimidate you, even cause you fear, no longer do.

It embarrasses me to see a karate fighter with a mushy body and a big gut hanging over his belt - especially if that belt is black. The uninformed sees that and judges all martial artists to be that way. I have heard non-martial artists say, upon seeing an out-of-shape black belt, "He's a black belt? Man, I could take that guy."

Take pride in your art and get into the best shape that you can. You will feel like a million dollars and you will have confidence to handle fearful situations.

5. FIND A MANTRA

Sometimes a proverb, a clever saying like a bumper sticker, can go right to the heart of an issue. You know when one works for you because it will make you sit up with a start and say, "Hey, I love that. I believe that. That works for me."

Here are a few proverbs on the subject of fear. If you don't see one you like here, keep looking until you find one that clicks with you. When you do, say it over and over every day. Make it a mantra because your subconscious mind will be listening.

• Caution is not cowardly. Carelessness is not courage - *anonymous*

• Man cannot discover new oceans unless he has the courage to lose sight of the shore - *Andre Gide*

• It takes courage to push yourself to places that you have never been before, to test your limits, to break through barriers. And the day came when the risk it took to remain tight inside the bud was more painful than the risk it took to blossom -*Anais Nin*

• When danger approaches, sing to it - *Arab proverb*

• You have to accept whatever comes and the only important thing is that you meet it with courage and with the best that you have to give - *Eleanor Roosevelt*

• The bravest thing you can do when you are not brave is to profess courage and act accordingly. -*Corra Harris*

• Courage is being scared to death - but saddling up anyway - *John Wayne*

• To dare is to lose one's footing momentarily. To not dare is to lose one's self - *Soren Kierkegaard*

• Come to the edge.
  No, we will fall.
  Come to the edge.
  No, we will fall.
  They came to the edge.
   He pushed them, and they flew - *Guillaume Appolinaire*

• Courage is resistance to fear, mastery of fear - not absence of fear - *Mark Twain*

• Courage is a special kind of knowledge; the knowledge of how to fear what ought to be feared and how not to fear what ought not to be feared - *David Ben-Gurion*

• Most of our obstacles would melt away if, instead of cowering before them, we would make up our minds to walk boldly through them - *Orison Swett Marden*

• Life shrinks or expands in proportion to one's courage - *Anais Nin*

• Courage is simply the willingness to be afraid and act anyway - *Robert Anthony*

• The bravest are surely those who have the clearest vision of what is before them, glory and danger alike, and yet notwithstanding, go out to meet it - *Thucydides*

• Courage is not the absence of fear but rather the judgment that something else is more important than fear -*Ambrose Redmoon*

to be Safe in Your Daily Life

Typically, when I teach a personal safety class and discuss various steps that people should take to increase their odds of getting through their day in one piece, there are always one or two folks who misunderstand what I'm advocating and say, "But I can't live that way. I can't go around always being afraid and always being worried."

I agree with them that being afraid is not the way people should live their lives, but being aware and alert is. My experience as a police officer showed me that many victims of crime, if not most, got ripped off, stomped and mayhemed because they were walking around with their head in the clouds. They were so mentally preoccupied with where they were going, where they had been or who they were talking with on their cell phones, that they broke one or more personal safety rules. This resulted in their cars being stolen, their purses snatched, their bodies violated, and, in some cases, their lives taken.

Here are 10 rules to live by that will make your life and your loved ones' lives safer. Think of these rules as what Bruce Lee called in his movie classic, *Enter the Dragon*, "the art of fighting without fighting."

I'm proud to say that since I began training in karate in 1965, I have never had to use my fighting art outside of my job as a police officer. During my 29 years in law enforcement I got into countless battles, but in my private life - not a one. Perhaps the biggest reason is because I have always followed these 10 rules.

1. STAY INFORMED

Watch the news, read the paper and go to community meetings so that you know when there are child molesters, burglars, gang members, and car thieves active in your neighborhood. Educate yourself as to how to avoid being a victim and what you should do when you are suddenly confronted by a predator. Think of your safety as an ongoing education, something you put into practice every day.

2. ALWAYS STAY ALERT AND AWARE

There are four zones of mental alertness and awareness that extend from total unawareness to complete involvement in a situation. Let's call them The White Zone, The Yellow Zone, The Orange Zone and The Red Zone. While alert people move from one zone to another as a situation dictates, far too many people fail to move at all because they are unaware and don't see a reason to.

It would seem that martial artists should be more aware of their environment than other people, but there are many who aren't. It's been my observation that those karate students who train just for the social aspect of belonging to a school, for sport competition, or just as a unique way to get into shape, don't think about street survival any more often than the average non-martial artist. However, those who train primarily for street self-defense, usually think in terms of personal safety in all areas of their lives.

Let's take a look at the four zones to see how they can help you get through your day in this crazy world. Let's begin with the most dangerous place of all: The White Zone.

White Zone

People who go through their day in the White Zone make excellent crime victims. Their noses are buried in books as they ride on public transportation, they walk the streets lost in their headphone music, they leave their baby alone in the car as they dash into the post office, and they lose themselves in a window display, completely unaware of a nearby group of loitering gang members.

Clearly, the White Zone is a place that leaves the door wide open to attack.

Yellow Zone

If you primarily train in karate for street survival, you probably already have a heightened sense of mental awareness. As you walk to your car, you are aware of all the places a threat could be hiding. You make note of the white van and that large tree that blocks your view, the dumpster where you have seen transients loitering in the past, and the darkened alleyway where you have noticed scruffy characters walking in and out.

Heightened mental awareness is what the Yellow Zone is all about.

Orange Zone

Things are getting a little froggy (a police expression meaning highly suspicious) in this zone. The good news is that because you are in the Yellow Zone, you are quick to perceive that something is not right.

You and a friend are talking on a street corner when you notice a couple of big guys a half block away talking noisily and making catcalls at passersby. Later, when you bid farewell to your friend and begin to leave, one of the rowdy guys steps into your path and gives you a snarl that would make a pitbull envious.

You perceive the danger because you are in a heightened state of mental awareness, The Yellow Zone. If you had been mentally dozing in the White Zone, you wouldn't have noticed or even heard the two rowdy guys at all. Then when one of them stepped in front of you and you realized you were in danger, *if* you realized you were in danger, you might have been so startled by the confrontation that you froze. I've seen this happen to people many times. Unfortunately, they discovered that it's a long trip from the slumbering White Zone to the Orange Zone. Some never completed the journey.

The Red Zone

When you are in this zone you are in the thick of things: The big thug who stepped into your path swings a wine bottle. From the Orange Zone, you are ready and your reaction is instantaneous: you block, punch, kick, whatever. But if you had been walking along dreamily in the White Zone, you would have been taken completely by surprise. The Red Zone is a long journey from obliviousness.

Stay mentally alert and be ready for anything. Stay in the Yellow Zone.

3. CONFIDENCE

In time, your martial arts skill will give you a load of confidence that people will sense, including would-be bullies. But even if you are just starting out in the fighting arts, you still want to put on an attitude of being in charge of yourself and your space. Predators seek people who look distracted, meek and unaware. When you appear confident - shoulders back, eyes taking in everything as you walk with assertiveness and purpose - predators will look elsewhere for an easier mark.

4. TRUST THAT VOICE IN YOUR HEAD THAT SAYS "DANGER! DANGER!"

I agree with Bruce Lee who said that there is no such thing as a sixth sense, but rather a sharpening of the five. Your senses are constantly taking in information and comparing it to similar information that has comprised your life experiences up to the present. Your senses recognize when something is out of the norm, when something just isn't right. They talk to you in a little voice that is wise. Listen to it because it just might save your life.

5. CARRY A CELL PHONE IN YOUR CAR

These things are saving a lot of lives. People use them to call for help when their boat is sinking, when their private plane has crashed, and when they are being followed or somehow threatened. Recently in Portland, a lady used her phone to call 9-1-1 from the trunk of a kidnapper's car.

6. KEEP YOUR HOME, AUTO AND OFFICE SECURE

Invest in high quality locks, an alarm system, and plant thorny bushes under your windows. These are just examples of the many things you can do to be secure in those places you spend time. There is a myriad of information on home, car, school and office safety in books, magazines, at your local police department, and on the Internet. Check out my book *How to Live Safely in a Dangerous World*, available on my web site. Take every measure you can to safeguard your person and space.

7. CARRY PROTECTION IN YOUR CAR

I carry my arnis stick between the seat and the door in my private car where I can quickly grab it. It's legal to carry such a weapon in Oregon, but if you are considering doing it, you should first find out what the law is where you live.

8. AVOID GANG MEMBERS AND OTHER UNDESIRABLES

Whenever I tell people to cross the street when they see a cluster of gang members on the sidewalk, there are always a few who get indignant and say something like, "It's my right to walk on that sidewalk."

It's true, you do have a right to the sidewalk, but you need to ask yourself if it's the smartest thing to do to continue walking toward people who have a history of violence. You need to ask if it's worth exercising your rights to get hassled, verbally assaulted or physically hurt.

Keep this in mind: Gang members get their power from their numbers. When two or more of them walk together, they see themselves as a mighty, fearless force. Chances are you will pass by them without incident.

But maybe not.

9. DON'T GET INVOLVED IN ROAD RAGE

Does that creep in the pickup who you want to force to the curb and kick in the chops have a gun on his seat? How about that guy who pulls up along side, flips you the finger and gestures for you to pull over? Does he have a gun? Since you have no idea whether anyone is armed at any given time - and more people are armed now than ever - that is enough reason to stay in your car and keep on going.

Once I was riding in a car on a San Francisco freeway with Professor Rick Alamany. Traffic in San Francisco is always horrific, but during the evening rush hour it's a battle royale of metal and rubber. After yet another near collision with yet another insanely aggressive Samurai driver, I asked the Professor how he controlled himself from getting out and thumping one of these lunatic motorists into the pavement.

"That's easy," he said, far too serenely for the driving conditions. "I don't make the drivers that important. They are only in my life for a few seconds and then they are gone forever. But if I get out and hurt one, he will be with me all the way through the court system, the law suit, and he might be there smiling as they haul me off to jail. Or he might hurt or kill me, or I might do it to him."

Don't make those crazy drivers that important, and soon they will be gone.

10. STAY IN SHAPE AND TRAIN HARD IN YOUR CHOSEN MARTIAL ART

The better your physical condition, the more confident you will feel, act and look, elements that make you undesirable to a predator. If he stupid enough to attack you in spite of these obvious signs, your well-honed blocks, punches and kicks give you a decided advantage.

Conclusion

Let me leave you with something Professor Remy Presas, founder of Modern Arnis told me many years ago. One day, I was in his class training hard for my black belt in his Filipino stick fighting art, when he motioned me over to him. He put one hand on my shoulder and poked my chest with his other hand.

"You know, Christensen," he half whispered, looking around as if to see if any of the other students were in ear shot, "if you train very hard . . . "

I leaned even closer to him, because I knew the master was about to pass on wisdom that was probably centuries old. No doubt, I thought in my big head, few people had ever heard what I was about to be told. I would promise him to guard the knowledge with my life and pass it on to only a select, worthy few - a couple of my senior students, my children.

The professor gave a quick glance over my shoulders and then behind him again. He continued in that same whispered, sage-dripping tone. "If you train very hard . . . "

Yes? I screamed in my mind. *If I train very hard . . . what?*

"... you will be very good."

Huh? That's it? I thought. That's the sage advice on how to develop masterful fighting ability?

I was profoundly disappointed. I was expecting something that would be a tad more life altering.

But a few days later, the importance of what he said suddenly struck me. No, they weren't mystical words or words steeped in hidden meaning. They were simple, yet deeply profound. Words not meant to be kept secret, but to be passed on.

If you train very hard, you will be very good.

And now I'm passing those words on to you.

ABOUT THE AUTHOR

Loren W. Christensen has been studying the martial arts since 1965. Over the years he has earned ten black belts, seven in karate, two in jujitsu, and one in arnis. As a karate competitor, he won more than 50 trophies in the black belt division.

This is Loren's 11th book on the fighting arts and his many articles have appeared in all the martial arts magazines. He was recently featured in the book *Who's Who in the American Teacher's Association of the Martial Arts.*

Loren's experience in law enforcement began in 1967 when he served in the army as a military policeman in the United States and in Vietnam. He joined the Portland (Oregon) Police Bureau in 1972 and while still a rookie on probation, he began teaching defensive tactics to officers. Over the years, he worked the training unit, the gang unit, dignitary body guarding, and all the precincts as a street officer.

Loren's pragmatic approach to the fighting arts was borne during his tour in Vietnam when he quickly discovered that the fancy techniques and stiff classical moves from his traditional system didn't work in Saigon's mean streets. When he returned home, he began searching out a realistic approach to fighting, one that would serve him during his long career in law enforcement.

He is now a full-time writer and a teacher of realistic martial arts to citizens and people in law enforcement.

Loren's web site is http://www.aracnet.com/~lwc123/

Index

NOTES

NOTES

OTHER BOOKS BY LOREN CHRISTENSEN

The following books are available on Loren's web site
LWC BOOKS http://www.aracnet.com/~lwc123/

<u>Martial Arts Related</u>

- Solo Training
- Solo Training 2
- Crouching Tiger
- Fighter's Fact Book 2
- The Fighter's Body
- Timing in the Fighting Arts
- Winning With American Kata
- Anything Goes
- The Way Alone
- Fighting Power
- The Mental Edge
- The Mental Edge, Revised
- Speed Training
- The Way of the Warrior

<u>Police Related</u>

- Police Defensive Tactics
- Skinhead Street Gangs
- Street Gangs
- Gangbangers
- Deadly Force Encounters
- Skid Row Beat
- Far Beyond Defensive Tactics
- How to Live Safely in a Dangerous World

Also Available from Turtle Press:

Boxing: Advanced Tactics and Strategies
Vital Leglocks
Grappler's Guide to Strangles and Chokes
Fighter's Fact Book 2
The Armlock Encyclopedia
Championship Sambo
Complete Taekwondo Poomse
Martial Arts Injury Care and Prevention
Timing for Martial Arts
Strength and Power Training
Complete Kickboxing
Ultimate Flexibility
Boxing: A 12 Week Course
The Fighter's Body: An Owner's Manual
The Science of Takedowns, Throws and Grappling for Self-defense
Fighting Science
Martial Arts Instructor's Desk Reference
Solo Training
Solo Training 2
A Los Angeles Bouncer's Guide to Practical Fighting
Conceptual Self-defense
Martial Arts After 40
Warrior Speed
The Martial Arts Training Diary for Kids
Teaching Martial Arts
Combat Strategy
The Art of Harmony
Total MindBody Training
1,001 Ways to Motivate Yourself and Others
Ultimate Fitness through Martial Arts
Taekwondo Kyorugi: Olympic Style Sparring

For more information:
Turtle Press
1-800-77-TURTL
e-mail: orders@turtlepress.com